The Best of Café Stories

By Jerry Guarino

Dedicated to David and Nancy

"What James Beard was to cooking, Jerry Guarino is to modern fiction."
Paul Soderberg (author of The Elephant Queen)

"50 Italian Pastries is a short story reader's culinary delight. Jerry Guarino's 50 slice of life pieces are filled with delightful takes on people, places and things that make America great. He infuses his stories with life's delights: good food, great music, fine drink, and the emotional roller coaster of interpersonal relationships. I found his work honest and filled with delightful irony. He is a keen observer of the human condition and a writer of obvious talent. He is a master at mirroring to his readers all their foibles, their fantasies and their forever quest to understand why the wheel of life turns as it does. Café Stories is short story telling at its best."
Wayne C. Long (author of Eye Candy, Flash in the Hand and Stories from the Edges)

"Jerry Guarino's sends his readers on a merry chase through a wild array of micro/flash fiction--humor, satire, and pathos. He artfully captures gentle souls and slick cons, the high brows and their unsuspecting victims in characters that step from the page to engage the reader. He finds the tiniest trait that creates zany folks the reader wants to protect or strangle. Often at the same time. Prepare for the surprise twist at the end. He gets you every time."
Myra H. McIlvain (author of Legacy)

"The stories in the collection are tightly told tales with engaging storylines and interesting characters. There are plenty of twists and turns, and plenty of characters to delight in (and some to despise)."
Nathaniel Tower (Pushcart Prize nominated author and editor of Bartleby Scopes literary magazine)

"Guarino's style is simple and consistently powerful, his storytelling a triumph of art over artifice."
Ben Price (editor at <u>Zouch Magazine and Miscellany</u> (Canada)

"Guarino is a writer you can enjoy without feeling guilty, and I strongly recommend his work."
Steven Miller (editor of <u>Leaning House Press</u>)

"Jerry's writing is consistently fresh and inventive. His stories grab from the beginning, and then hurl the reader into surprising and powerful endings. Definitely a must-read. The Rich are Going to Hell, The Devil's Orchestra and The Grand Poobah are some of my favorite Guarino pieces. Always inventive, Jerry Guarino is one of my favorite short story writers. His work hooks you from the first sentence and doesn't let go until you reach the end, making this one writer you won't forget."
Earl Wynn (editor of <u>Weirdyear</u>, <u>Daily Love</u> and <u>Yesteryear Fiction</u>)

"I found myself intertwined in the lives of each character, not knowing until the end that every one of them held a magical piece to the puzzle we call human nature; the larger picture of which only became clear after reading the final word. This collection of shorts is something that avid fans of storytelling should go out of their way to find."
Jim Idema (screenwriter and author)

"Jerry Guarino's writing reminds me of the late, but great, Jose Saramago's. His structure is both unique and compelling, always leading the reader to places that they never see coming."
Weeb Heinrich (editor of <u>Writing Raw</u>)

"Jerry Guarino's stories are a real treat for the reader. Each story is well crafted with the natural elegance of a natural writer. <u>The Fringe Magazine</u> has enjoyed his short stories and has had the pleasure of publishing these gems for the past year."
Scott Wilson (editor of <u>The Fringe Magazine</u> (Australia)

"The beauty in Jerry's work is the ease with which he breaks that serious concentration without sacrificing quality. Preheat the Microwave.Com has a relevant, poignant subject at its heart but it is delivered to the reader with eloquent comedy."
Jenny Catlin (editor of Scissors and Spackle)

"Jerry Guarino takes the nuances of everyday, places it on its head, and then tilts it slightly to the left. His comical spin on life will make you wheeze with mirth and leave you wanting more."
Daniel Poole (editor of Larks Fiction Magazine)

"I loved Jerry's short stories and his choice of words. These little tales are great! He has a way with words and pulling you into the story, wanting more! My one and only complaint was when the book ended. I wanted there to be 50 more short stories."
Reyna Hawk (author of Angels and Arrows and Looking Through Blind Eyes)

"Jerry Guarino has a knack for looking past the social illusions that poison our world."
Sand Pilarski (managing editor of The Piker Press)

"Jerry Guarino's writing is refreshing and authentic. His storytelling grasps the nuances of life, leading the reader into expertly crafted moments of intimacy, humor, thoughtfulness, and surprise. Read one story and you're hooked. "50 Italian Pastries" is a delicious read! He knows how to tell a story and with this collection, one finds bite-sized nuggets that heartily fulfill any reader's palate for variety! Guarino is a connoisseur with words, flavoring his stories with the seasonings of life, including laughter, loss, revelation, insight and wisdom. Go ahead, dig in. You'll enjoy every bite, I mean, story."
Sheila Pierson (author of Steak and Potatoes)

Table of Contents

The 7 Hills Technology Group is the second in the series of Detective Tony Mariani Mysteries, a sequel to The Da Vinci Diamond.

The 7 Hills Technology Group

Chapter 1

Captain Williams briefs Detective Mariani and his assistant, Officer Pam Johnson on The 7 Hills Technology Group (7HTG), a highly classified company of scientists working for the government.

"The next case may require even more technology expertise than The Da Vinci Diamond; this one involves threats against a high tech firm."

"Which company Captain?"

"The 7 Hills Technology Group, based in San Francisco. They noticed anonymous threats against their technology. I want you to go meet with them today."

"Who are they?"

"Sort of combination think tank and intelligence unit. They report to the NSA, FBI and CIA. Their technology is classified top secret."

"Sounds like a job for federal authorities, doesn't it?"

"Normally, yes, but they want us to support them in gathering information, in case this spills over to San Francisco. Don't worry; the FBI is the point agency for now. You'll just be working with them."

"Anyone we know?"

"Glad you asked. Agent Jenny Moore just transferred from the New York office to San Francisco. The FBI and I thought you did such a good job before that you could work well again on this one."

"That's fine Captain. When does she arrive?"

"She'll be here in about an hour. You're going to the 7HTG office together. But Tony, there's one more important point."

"Yes, Captain?"

"Their building is a SCIF, electronically secured. You won't be able to use cell phones or any electronics while you're in there. If you need to contact us, you're going to have to leave the building."

"Sounds more interesting by the minute. All right Captain. I hope we don't have to go there with hoods over our heads."

The captain smiles. "No, but your files and meetings will have to be secured. The only people cleared are you, Pam, Dr. Lee and myself."

"Will we need Dr. Lee today?"

"No, there are no dead bodies or crime scenes yet."

"Yet?"

"Trust me. This one might get messy. Agent Moore will brief you on the way to the meeting."

"Pam, start a file on our system. Secure it with encryption, and then come back here to go to the meeting. We will only be able to make paper notes at their site, then you'll transfer what we learn into the electronic file when we get back."

"Yes detective."

Within the hour, Mariani and Johnson were riding with Agent Jenny Moore to 7HTG. Agent Moore is briefing them.

"It's good to be working with you two again. When the opening came up in San Francisco, I jumped on it."

"You'll like it here Agent Moore," said Tony.

"Please call me Jenny when we're in private. You too Officer Johnson."

"Thank you Jenny," said Pam.

Mariani raises a finger. "Jenny, if this group is so highly classified, why are they letting us investigate?"

"Good question. The NSA is working on it from Washington. They needed someone to work the streets, someone with local jurisdiction. The CIA isn't allowed to work in the U.S., but we are. I'm here to filter information between you and the government."

"And filter information from them to us?"

"Yes, unfortunately. There are parts of this case that you won't be read in on. I'll review all your findings and pass them up to the appropriate agency. You'll get information back on a need to know basis."

"Hmm. Let's hope they trust us."

"You and Pam were background checked last month. You have the equivalent of FBI clearance for this case. Just don't start writing any bad checks." Mariani and Johnson laugh.

Moore turns off Fulton Street into Golden Gate Park, and then pulls the car up to a windmill. "Here we are."

Mariani looks around. "The windmill. It's just a Dutch relic from the early 1900s. This can't be where a secret technology group works."

"Not exactly. Their offices are below ground. Four thousand feet of secrecy in the heart of Golden Gate Park. Follow me. Oh, but leave your cell phones locked in the trunk."

Moore, Mariani and Johnson walk up to the windmill. Moore taps a nine-digit code into a keypad and an iron gate opens to let them in. When it closes, another secure door opens to reveal an elevator. They get in and wait.

"Don't you have to push a floor number or talk to someone?" said Johnson.

"Do you see floor numbers? No, they already know who we are; there are audio microphones and video cameras outside. They have been following us since we parked."

Moore was right. The elevator showed three buttons, but no indication of a floor. When the elevator stopped, Robert Sanders greeted them.

"Welcome Agent Moore. It's nice to meet you Detective Mariani and Officer Johnson. Please follow me."

Sanders led them to a small conference room. "Please take a seat."

Sanders pushed a button next to the light switch. The glass frosted over and a low hum sounded. A blue light circled the top of the room, indicating they were now inside a SCIF. Detective Mariani offered his hand.

"Mr. Sanders, I'm Detective Mariani from the San Francisco Police Department."

"Yes detective. We know who you are, as well as Officer Johnson and FBI Agent Moore."

"Of course you do. Then perhaps you can tell us why we're here."

"Glad to. We have been getting disturbing messages electronically and by telephone."

"What kind of messages, Mr. Sanders?"

"Random short messages referring to projects we are working on for the government. Our engineers have not seen any data compromised and we have swept for signs of a hacker, but nothing."

"What specific messages sir?"

"As I said, pop up lines on engineer screens referring to projects. I can't tell you the specific message. The code name is classified."

"Then I'm not sure what we can do to help. Do you think the leak may be coming from inside the company?"

"That's possible, but all of our people have top secret clearance, verified by the FBI and NSA."

"When did this start?"

"Our first notice was a week ago."

"Did you hire anyone new lately?"

"No. Our last hire was six months ago."

"I don't suppose you can give me a list of the employees."

"I'm afraid not. We protect their identity so they can't be compromised by outside agents."

"Mr. Sanders. What would you like us to do?"

"Detective. I know this seems like an impossible situation. We were hoping you might be able to use your resources to investigate a person that we suspect might be involved."

"And who is that please?"

"Lisa Appleton."

"Does she work here?"

"No sir. She's an escort in San Francisco. We have been tracking her social media conversations and she has referred to liaisons with two of our engineers. So you can see why we can't get involved with this person directly. We thought local law enforcement was the best way to start."

"Do you have an address or phone number for Miss Appleton."

Sanders hands Mariani a paper with her name, address and phone number, along with the name of the escort service. "Here you are."

"All right Mr. Sanders. We'll look into it. But espionage is really the role of the FBI, not local law enforcement."

"I understand, but you know San Francisco better than they do. That's why you're working with Agent Moore."

"We'll certainly look into it. Thank you."

"Thank you, detective."

Sanders escorts Mariani, Johnson and Moore out of the building. On the way back to the San Francisco Police Department, Moore discusses their next step.

"Tony, I know this is unusual."

"Unusual? It's right out of some spy novel. So Mr. Sanders wants us to investigate an escort who might have compromised one of his engineers."

"Yes, that's about it."

"Pam, you were taking notes. Is that all?"

"Except that their servers were compromised without any sign of hackers yes."

"All right. And we don't know the names of the engineers or anyone else at 7HTG except for Robert Sanders."

"Yes sir."

Mariani turns back to Agent Moore. "And is that all you know too Jenny?"

"Yes Tony. I'm sorry."

"OK, we'll follow Miss Appleton and see if we can get an idea of how she is involved."

"Thanks. I'll be in touch."

Agent Moore drops Mariani and Johnson off at SFPD, and then heads back to the San Francisco FBI office.

"Pam, document your notes and keep them encrypted. I'll brief the captain. Then see what you can find about Miss Appleton."

"Yes detective."

Chapter 2

Noria Park is preparing a gourmet dinner for her boyfriend Robert Sanders. Noria is quite stunning, with blended traits from her Korean father and Italian mother. With long, dark hair, brown eyes, a model's face and athletic 5'10" frame, she stopped traffic everywhere she went. After completing a degree in business from Stanford, she became an analyst for a San Francisco investment firm, specializing in technology.

"I'm home dear. How was your day?"

"You know I took today off to cook for you sweetheart. What about your day, or is it classified?"

"Everything's classified Noria. But we did have some visitors."

"Oh, who was that?"

"A San Francisco detective. You would like him, name is Tony Mariani."

"And why was he visiting you?"

"I'm afraid that's all I can say." He puts his arms around Noria from the back while she is stirring sauce.

"Robert James Sanders. I don't know why I stay with you. Next time just don't tell me anything." She pouts and pushes him away.

"Don't be like that dear. I brought you something."

Noria raises an eyebrow. "OK, what?"

Sanders pulls out a jewelry case. He opens it to reveal a silver necklace holding a heart shaped pendant with a ruby in the center. "Here." He puts it over her head. "Now am I forgiven?"

"For now." She looks at the necklace in the reflection of one of her stainless steel pans. "You remembered I like rubies. Government work must be paying better than I thought."

"Well..." Sanders begins to say.

"I know. Classified. Now if you could only find some matching earrings, I'd be ready for the opera." She continues to admire her necklace. "You know, I analyze tech firms each day, but your company doesn't show up anywhere. Maybe you're just a CIA agent."

Sanders turns her around and gives her a long, passionate kiss. Noria presses her body against his. After a minute, she pushes him away.

"No, not a CIA agent. They don't kiss that well. Now let me put dinner on the table or we'll never get to dessert."

"All right. I'll go start a fire. We can eat in the living room." Sanders turns on the gas fireplace, reflecting romantic light in the oversized front window, overlooking San Francisco Bay. Then he sets two place settings on the teakwood coffee table. The third floor condo in the Marina District provided a view of The Golden Gate Bridge but also the privacy they would need for an intimate dinner.

Bob Sanders had everything he wanted. A prestigious job with a tech company working on classified government projects, a gorgeous twenty-seven year old girlfriend and a home in one of the most exclusive neighborhoods of San Francisco. Now, he just had to plug the leak in his company before some sensitive information got out.

Chapter 3

Johnson wasted no time doing a background check on Lisa Appleton. She went into Mariani's office to tell him.

"Detective. Lisa Appleton is not your average hooker. She has a degree in Art History from Cal and grew up in Mill Valley in a respectable, upper class family. I'm not even sure her parents know what she does now."

"Hmm. And where is the escort service?"

"It's run out of the Richmond district. But it's strictly outcall. They meet their clients in hotels around the city, never where the girls live."

"All right. Let's see if we can follow Miss Appleton. Do you know where she lives?"

"Yes. 2845 Ocean View Drive in Pacifica. It's a condo. She doesn't have a land line, but I have her cell phone number."

"Very good Pam. We'll put a car out by her condo and when she comes out, you and I will follow her around tomorrow. Meanwhile, have someone in vice look into the escort service, to see if they have anything."

"Will do. Is that all for today?"

"Well, yes. But you must be hungry. Want to go out for a pizza?"

"Sure, but is that OK?"

"Hey, I go out with David all the time; and other officers too. It's in public, no conflicts of interest here. Why?"

Pam gives him a *'you know'* look, then whispers. "Rome."

Tony also lowers his voice. "Yes, a beautiful city. Why don't we talk about it over a pie?" Then he smiles.

"All right, all right," said Pam. "Just let me change out of my uniform. I'll meet you in about ten minutes."

"Good. I'll wait out front."

When they arrive at Tony's favorite pizza grill, the hostess, a nice Italian lady from the neighborhood, greets them.

"Detective Tony. Welcome. We haven't seen you in a while."
"Sorry Rosa. We've been pretty busy. Did I tell you we were in Rome last month?"

"Oh. Roma. I was born there. Did you take any pictures?"

"Yes, but none that you would like, just crime scenes. Did you hear about The Da Vinci Diamond?"

"Si, Si Tony. Were you working on that?"

"In a way Rosa. Listen, we can chat later; can you put on a pie and bring us a basket of Chianti?"

"Of course, Tony. Take a seat over there."

"Grazi, Rosa. Pam, let's have some dinner."

Tony and Pam take the corner booth, away from the noise in the kitchen. On top of the checkered tablecloth were flowers and a romantic, red candle burning. The waitress brought them the basket of wine and poured it into two glasses.

"You know David and I have the same meal here when we can. My cousin owns this place. We're safe here."

"I mean. What about the other thing? You know," said Pam.

"The romance? Do you regret that?"

"No, no. In fact I'm..."

"What Pam?"

"I'm more sure than I was then that this felt right."

"I'm glad to hear that. I felt the same way. We really seem to have something good. We can stop it cold or..."

"Or what Tony?"

"Or we could see how it goes, or..."

"Oh. You mean see each other secretly?"

"Yes, if that's what you would like."

Pam brushed the hair from her face, and then smiled. "I would like that. But what if someone finds out?"

"Pam, I'm a senior detective. I know how to keep secrets. I'm sure you can too."

"Well, yes. I can be discreet."

Tony takes her hand under the table. "Fine, then let's try that. We maintain a completely professional relationship at work and keep our private life private. Come and go at different times. Meet with David or other officers outside. You know, act like colleagues, not lovers."

"But what if the worst happened? If somebody did find out?"

"The worst case is that they would ask us to stop seeing each other or transfer out. If that happened, do you think you could transfer to another precinct in the city?"

"Yes, I think I could." Pam smiled at Tony. "Guess I better pick up one of my uniforms to leave at your home."

Tony smiled. "Yes, that makes sense. And some personal items."

Tony felt love just like he had with Pam in Rome. Before that it had been over a year since his wife died in a car accident. The chemistry he and Pam had renewed his energy and focus. Pam was clearly looking for more than an affair and that was fine with him. They had dinner. When they were ready to leave, Pam excused herself to the ladies room.

Rosa caught Tony by the door. "She's very beautiful Tony. Like Beth."

"Thank you Rosa." Tony kisses her on the cheek. "Tell the chef the pie was perfect."

Tony and Pam continued the romance they started in Rome, each hoping it would last.

Chapter 4

After dining on fresh caprese salad, eggplant cannelloni and veal piccata, a bottle of Chianti and jazz music, Bob and Noria were now quite mellow.

While he was dreaming of the love to come, Noria took the dishes to the kitchen.

"Don't leave."

"I'll be right back," she said.

Sanders gazed out his window at San Francisco Bay and the stars above. It was ample compensation for his stressful job and the secrets he had to keep. Here he could relax and forget about work.

Noria came out of the bedroom, carrying a tray with candles and a mink glove she had bought for her lover. She was wearing a short, red satin kimono with decorative flowers and not much else. Her hair fell seductively around her shoulders and she was wearing the necklace he had given her. She was barefoot and her red painted nails shone in the light from the fire.

"I bought you something too sweetheart." She handed him the mink glove. Her glance was all the encouragement he needed.

He took off his clothing and lay down with her on the bearskin rug in front of the fire. The stars twinkled outside and the fire danced in front of them. Candles and jazz music completed the mood.

Stripped down to his underwear, he started to kiss Noria while stroking her with the mink glove. She turned over and pulled up her kimono enough to reveal her back. "Rub my back please."

He obeyed with long, slow strokes across the small of her back, then down the back of her legs, feet, and ankles and along the inside and outside of her thigh.

"Mmm," she moaned as he brought the glove near her mound. "Not yet lover. You haven't done the other side."

Noria rolled over on her back and opened the kimono. There he could see two perfect thirty-six inch breasts, a flat stomach with a belly button ring and a ruby in it matching her necklace. She closed her eyes and continued to direct him.

"Now slowly massage me."

He started the glove on the front of her feet, then legs, pausing around her pleasure just enough to elicit more moans. From there he slid the glove to her sides, stomach and finally under and around her breasts.

"Ooh. Ooh. Don't stop. Kiss me."

Bob kissed her slowly. While his left hand gently cupped around her neck, his right hand continued to massage her breasts with the glove. Noria reached down to her vagina and began massaging herself.

He couldn't stand the slow pace and positioned himself between her legs to relieve her fingers with his tongue. Within a few minutes, she was having her first orgasm.

"Oh, Bob. Yes. More."

Bob continued performing on her while she came. When she was done, she opened her eyes and looked up.

"Your turn." The wicked smile accompanied an aggressive throw of him over onto his back. She began licking him all over.

"Ooh. Yes," he said as she reached his member.

Noria took long, very slow motions to him with her mouth, just pausing enough to increase the intensity he felt. She reached up with her other hand to put her finger into his mouth so they were both sucking at the same time. She teased his tongue with her finger while driving him to ecstasy with her tongue. Sensing he couldn't take any more, she slid on top of him and rode him. He held her breasts and they both came together.

Chapter 5

On Saturday morning, Agent Moore calls Mariani to set up a meeting. "Tony, this is Jenny."

"Yes Jenny. Any news you can share?"

"Yes, but not over the phone."

"Of course not. OK, where should we meet?"

"I'll come down to the station this morning around ten o'clock."

"See you there. We'll meet in Captain Williams' office."

"See you soon."

Tony turned back over to bed and woke up Pam. "We have a meeting at the station in an hour."

"An hour? Guess I should get into the shower," she said demurely.

"Not yet dear" said Tony. He pulled off her panties, lifted her legs above him and entered her for a quickie.

"Oh, Tony. Yes. Push harder."

Tony obeyed with all the vigor of someone half his age. His 24-year-old lover made it easy for him to feel young. After ten minutes he came and led Pam to the shower where they continued massaging each other. Positioned behind her while soaping her body, Pam began to get excited. She brought herself to orgasm while he held her. Then they cleaned up, dressed and left for the precinct.

Tony dropped her off a few blocks away. She was already in the uniform she left at Tony's apartment. Tony walked in first, followed by Pam ten minutes later.

Dr. Lee greets Tony at the door. "I heard we're meeting with Agent Moore, Tony."

"That's right. She'll be here soon. She told me she has an update."

"Good, this case needs more information."

When Agent Moore arrives, they get started.

"Well, we're getting a little more information from 7HTG now. They told me which employee they expect is sleeping with Lisa Appleton. It's Ted Eisenberg, a software engineer and expert at encrypting files."

"Do they think he's behind the messages?"

"Perhaps, but maybe you can find out from Appleton. Eisenberg is playing it cool at work, no suspicious behavior."

"Well, we have been following Appleton. She likes to meet with clients at the more exclusive hotels. She must be pulling in some clients with serious money. Those rooms don't rent by the hour, more like $500 a day and up. We haven't seen Eisenberg yet but I doubt he could afford her and the hotel room on a regular basis."

Agent Moore nods in agreement. "You're right detective. We ran his financials; he must be getting the informant rate. But keep following him. We're going to get a wire tap and start recording his phone calls."

"Without probable cause?" said Captain Williams.

"It's within the discretion of FISA warrants. We have a lot of latitude since 911."

"But this isn't a foreign intelligence matter."

Agent Moore smiles. "Actually, it could be. That's all I can say."

"Have they given you any more information?"

"Yes, they asked if we could take a look at Jan Sawyer, another engineer there."

"Why do they suspect her?"

"Well, she has been dating Eisenberg on and off for the last year."

"Do you have her address?"

"Yes, here it is, along with her cell phone number. She lives near the park."

"All right. We'll add her to the surveillance."

Captain Williams looks to Agent Moore. "These hours are adding up agent. Can we expect some reimbursement from the FBI?"

"I'm glad you mentioned that Captain. Here is a log form. Just note the man hours and other expenses and we'll be picking up the tab."

Williams looks at Mariani. "Well, can you believe that Tony?"
"The feds offering to pay for our expenses; this is a first."

"Still I don't want you spending all your time following Eisenberg and Sawyer. Put some junior officers on them and they can report to you. No need to read them in on why they are being followed. You just get involved if they do anything suspicious."

"Will do captain." Tony looks at Agent Moore. "Jenny, has 7HTG learned anything more about the messages appearing on the monitors."

"Yes. I still can't give you the project code names, but they said there was a message that this project was referred to as coming to an end soon."

"Ominous or a hoax?"

"They are taking it very seriously and if you knew what the project was, you would be too."

"Can you give us a hint?"

"All I can say is that it involves technology that would be of great interest to Asian countries not aligned with the U.S."

"So North Korea and China?"

"Yes."

"Yes, both or yes one of them."

"Yes."

Mariani just shook his head at all the cloak and dagger. "All right, I'll assume it's either North Korea or China and that it's probably technology that involves military or intelligence data."

Moore puts her hand to her forehead in a matter to suggest she has said too much. "I've got to watch myself around you Tony."

"Don't worry. I'm a patriot and can be trusted. So can my team. You won't find any leaks here." Dr. Lee and Officer Johnson nod in agreement.

"Good. It's my head that will fall if any of this gets out. National security is like that." A ping goes off on Agent Moore's phone. "I just got a message from one of my agents about Ted Eisenberg. Looks like he's planning to meet Lisa Appleton tonight."

"Did it say where?"

"At Scoma's restaurant on Fisherman's Wharf at six for dinner; then he has a reservation at the Mark Hopkins hotel for the night, room 223."

"Sounds expensive. How much does Eisenberg make?"

"Only $55,000. Guess he's going into debt for Miss Appleton."

Tony holds up Lisa's picture, a drop dead gorgeous blonde around 5'9", 130 pounds with a model's face. "May I remind you he's a 25 year old computer nerd and he's sleeping with this? Some people gamble, some people do drugs. Eisenberg spends his money on her."

Moore comments. "Still, that's a pretty steep price for a date, even for Miss Appleton."

Dr. Lee agrees. "Yeah Tony. Doesn't smell right. How long has Eisenberg been seeing Lisa Appleton?"

"According to the FBI, once a week for the past three months."

"Then he's definitely getting a long term discount or they are meeting for some other reason. Could be Appleton is getting Intel from Eisenberg. Does he even know she's a professional?"

"We don't know yet. It may be that he's deluded himself into thinking that they are just dating. Young men have a strong ability to suspend disbelief, but this would take naiveté to a new level."

Agent Moore responds. "Well, we'll know soon enough. We've reserved the room next door to them and have a surveillance team setting up there now."

Captain Williams questions. "Agent Moore, can Tony and Pam stay in room 221 instead of your agents?"

"Yes, I think that may be better. Plain clothes. The tech will be with you in the room recording and reporting, but no other agents to tip them off. You and Johnson go to Scoma's for dinner, and then follow them back to the hotel. Make sure you're carrying some tourist items in case they spot you."

"Right. Ghirardelli Square shopping bag and San Francisco fleece sweaters."

Chapter 6

Mariani and Johnson arrived at the restaurant about the same time as Eisenberg and Appleton. They were hoping to sit close enough to hear their conversation but they were seated a few tables away, close enough to observe, but not to hear.

Tony gives Pam final instructions. "Remember Pam, we're two tourists in town for dinner and a fancy hotel."

Pam gets into character immediately. "Tony, wasn't that boat ride wonderful? The cool air made me so hungry. This looks like a great restaurant."

Tony realized he wouldn't have to worry about Pam's cover. "Yes dear, it's highly regarded around here. Like Legal Seafood back in Boston."

Meanwhile Ted Eisenberg held Lisa's chair out and they sat down. As they read the menus, Ted held her hand. She smiled and circled her finger inside his palm. Ted had the look of an engineer who just won the lottery, but with love, not money.

"What do you like tonight?" said Lisa.

"I think I'd like that salmon with fresh vegetables dear. What about you?"

"The crab Louie salad. Maybe with some chowder."

Tony noticed this small talk and whispered to Pam. "Nothing unusual yet, except for the fact that she is way out of his league."

Pam replied back in character. "Why dear, that's lovely, yes I think I will have the Australian lobster with white wine sauce. Are you going to get it too?"

"Not this time love. I think I'll get the Alaskan king crab and steak combo."

Well, dinner didn't reveal anything new to the detective and officer. They appeared to be a tourist couple out for dinner. Mariani tried to time their exit so they could follow Eisenberg from the restaurant. Before that, Lisa excused herself to go to the ladies room. Pam followed a minute later.

In the bathroom, Pam commented on Lisa's outfit. "My that's a gorgeous dress. Did you buy it here?"

Lisa returned the compliment. "Why yes. At Belljar on 16th Street. You look lovely too. Are you visiting San Francisco?"

"Yes, my boyfriend and I are from Boston. I think he's going to propose this weekend." Pam played the excited tourist so well that Lisa dropped any suspicions.

"Oh, that's nice. I saw you at the table across from us. He's very handsome. Where did you meet?"

"In Rome actually. We were both there on vacation and met in a museum."

"How romantic. And you're both from Boston?"

"Yes. Tony is a college professor and I'm a librarian. My name is Pam." She extended her hand to Lisa.

"My name's Lisa. Nice to meet you. Sounds like a match made in heaven. Where are you staying?"

"The Mark Hopkins. We heard it was very nice."

"You don't say. We're staying there tonight too. You'll love it. The rooms are exquisite. Well, I have to get back to my date. Best of luck this weekend."

Pam didn't want to pry about Eisenberg. Instead she just played along. "You too Lisa." Lisa went back to her table. A minute later Pam joined Tony. Both men were paying the checks.

Pam whispered to Tony, as if they were trading love secrets. "She called him her date and is wearing a thousand dollar dress."

"How do you know?"

"Women know Tony." They let Ted and Lisa leave the restaurant first, knowing that a plain clothes FBI agent outside the restaurant would be following them.

Tony and Pam let Ted and Lisa get ahead of them so that they wouldn't be detected any more that night. The agent trailing Eisenberg and Appleton let Tony know after they had checked in to the room. Then Tony and Pam went up to their room, opened the door and saw the FBI tech listening to room 223.

Tony and Pam put down their coats and bag and pulled up a chair next to the tech. "Anything yet?" said Tony.

"Well, Lisa said they met a lovely couple from Boston. Playing it kind of close aren't you guys?"

Pam said. "I was hoping to get a feel for their relationship. Did I mess up?"

Tony replied. "No Pam, you're doing fine. This is what happens to normal couples. It would have been more suspicious if we tried to follow them without connecting."

"Probably true," said the tech. "We should know a lot more after tonight."

It wasn't long before they saw Ted undressing Lisa. Her experience as a prostitute was apparent by the way she made Ted feel like he was her boyfriend. Within the hour they were in passionate positions. Pam felt a little embarrassed watching and listening, but Tony and the tech maintained a professional demeanor.

After the climaxes, the tech could hear Ted talking with Lisa. The tech took off his headphones and then turned up the speaker just enough so Tony and Pam could hear. "Listen to this guys."

"So Ted. What's new at work?"

"You know darling. All that secret, boring tech stuff."

"Sweetheart, I think it's exciting what you do. Tell me about it?"

"Well, I am working with something interesting. Have you heard of drones?"

"You mean those little airplanes?" Lisa inquired innocently.

"Yes, the little airplanes. I'm writing some code so that people can't hack into them. Encryption."

"How neat. Do you get to see the airplanes fly?"

"Yes, we get video feeds from their camera to make sure our code is working properly."

"And where do they fly darling?" Lisa back in her negligee, showing off her beautiful body rubbed the back of Ted's neck and kissed him on the cheek.

"That's classified dear. Sorry."

Lisa moved her hand down to his chest. She could sense Ted's enthusiasm returning. "Oh." She gave him a little pout while continuing to excite him.

Ted gave in. "These drones fly in Asia. But that's all I can say."

Lisa rewarded his mistake by giving him a long kiss. "My little techie boyfriend. So you're trying to protect the drones from terrorists?"

"Something like that. These drones have become quite common around the world, especially in the Middle East, supporting our troops."

The tech gave Tony and Pam a look. "That's enough for us to detain Mr. Eisenberg. I'm going to leave the recorder on and report. I'll be back in the morning to pick it up."

"So we should stay here?" said Pam.

"Yes, we'll give you a call after they leave in the morning. We would prefer that you don't run into them by accident, but it would be suspicious if they wanted to meet you for breakfast and you had already checked out. Enjoy the room."

"All right," said Tony. The FBI tech left to tell Agent Moore about the confession and prepare to arrest Eisenberg in the morning.

Tony looked at Pam, realizing they had had an exciting undercover assignment and were now alone in a fancy hotel. Pam was first to speak.

"I guess we should get some rest. We'll have to meet with Agent Moore tomorrow." She began to take off her dress.

Tony got the message. "Yes, Pam. I'm kind of tired myself," all the while realizing the romantic opportunity to come, all on the FBI's dime. "Nice hotel room."

"Lovely bed and view."

"Wonder if they have some music. Why yes, they do. What do you like dear?"

"Any Andrea Bocelli?" remembering their time in Rome.

"How about that. Yes." Tony put the Bocelli CD in the Bose stereo and also put a Diana Krall CD in the queue.

Tony and Pam recreated their time in Rome with a night of romantic passion. It was a little dangerous to be involved this way in the middle of a surveillance mission, but they were just playing their part. No reason to go into details with anyone else. No one would be interrupting them in the hotel.

They alternately slept and made love until seven o'clock, then noticed a light blinking on the phone.

Just as the tech had predicted, Lisa had left a message at their room to meet them for breakfast. The FBI was waiting outside the hotel to pick up Eisenberg.

Tony and Pam saw Ted and Lisa at a corner table of the restaurant. Lisa made the introductions. "Ted, this is Pam and Tony. They are from Boston."

Ted shook hands with them both. "So nice to meet you. How are you enjoying San Francisco?"

Tony answered. "You know it's a little like Boston. Waterfront, great seafood and winding streets."

Ted added. "But I'll bet you don't have these steep hills, like the one from the restaurant to the hotel."

"No, that was pretty intense. Good thing we took the trolley car. We wouldn't have made it up that hill after dinner."

Lisa joined in. "Tony what do you teach in Boston?"

"English literature. Ted, what do you do?"

"Oh, I'm just a techie nerd. Programming."

With this comment, the disparity between Ted and Lisa was even more obvious. Tony and Pam had difficulty not questioning more about their relationship for fear of prying too much.

"We have a lot of tech firms in Boston too. And great universities. MIT, Harvard, Boston University."

Ted said. "Yes, we have some people from those schools at our shop. I went to MIT myself."

"What about you Lisa? What do you do?"

"I'm in public relations. I studied Art History at Cal."

"So you're a local girl?"

"Pretty much. I grew up in Marin County. You too should get up there this weekend. There are some very romantic places," hinting to Pam that she might find the perfect spot for Tony's proposal. Fortunately, Pam had disclosed her conversation with Lisa to Tony.

"Where would you suggest Lisa?" said Tony.

"Well, you can get out to the coast, Bodega Bay or up to wine country within an hour."

"Thank you Lisa. We'll check it out. Right dear?"

Pam cuddled into Tony's arm. "Yes, that sounds wonderful."

After breakfast, the couples said goodbye. Lisa took her BMW back home and as Tony and Pam got into a cab for the SFPD, FBI agents took Eisenberg away in a black SUV for questioning.

Chapter 7

Noria Park was going over her notes on the computer. She sent a text message to Lisa Appleton.

Lisa. Did you get anything else from Eisenberg yesterday?

Within a minute she got a response.

Yes Noria. He's working on encrypting drones flying in Asia.

Did he say where in Asia?

No, not yet. But I'll get it out of him next time. Can't go too fast with this one.

All right, stay on him. Do you need any money?

Not right now. I can wait for my allowance.

Very good. I'll be in touch.

Noria had Appleton working the 7HTG engineer for a few months now and already had sensitive Intel on their technology. Now she just had to work her other contact, Jan Sawyer, to continue leaving misinformation on the company computers.

All the while she worked Appleton to get Intel from Eisenberg, she was working Sanders from within his condo. Sanders had no idea that Noria was a North Korean agent or what she was running with Appleton and Eisenberg. His whole department was being compromised and he didn't realize it. Moreover, Noria and Sanders didn't know that the FBI picked up Eisenberg and was questioning him now about his indiscretions with Appleton.

Chapter 8

The next day, Agent Moore and Detective Mariani met with Robert Sanders at 7HTG. Once they were safely inside the SCIF, Moore revealed the information Sanders was dreading to hear.

"Mr. Sanders, I'm afraid our surveillance of Ted Eisenberg caught him discussing information about your projects with Lisa Appleton."

"Can you tell me to what extent?"

"He told her he worked on encrypting drones that fly in Asia. From our interrogation of him, we don't think he said anything else."

"Needless to say, that was enough. We'll have to fire him immediately and remove his clearance. What are you going to do?"

"We consider this very serious, Mr. Sanders, a breach of classified information to an outside party. We're going to bring in Miss Appleton for questioning. We'll hold Eisenberg until we confirm the extent of their conversations. In any event, we have enough to charge him with espionage."

"What about Jan Sawyer? She was dating Ted. Do you think she's involved?"

"Since she has access to all the classified information he had, we don't think so. There are no indications that Ms. Sawyer was communicating with Lisa Appleton, but we're going to keep her under surveillance nonetheless. Once she learns that Ted has been fired, they may talk, but that won't be for a while yet; he will be in custody until a trial."

"We'll let the staff know that Ted was let go, but not go into details. The NSA will have to know about this, won't they?"

Agent Moore nods. "I'm afraid so sir. Let's hope this doesn't effect your project status or contracts with them."

"This is terrible. Let's hope that Ted was the only one involved. We'll change all our passwords and security protocols immediately. I'll contact the NSA and give them a report. They've been very happy with our work, so I'm hoping we can contain this."

"We hope so too Mr. Sanders. Detective Mariani will continue to monitor Miss Appleton and Jan Sawyer, secretly of course. If he finds anything else, we'll let you know."

"Thank you Detective. And thank you Agent Moore."

Chapter 9

One of Noria's informants was keeping tabs on Eisenberg. He called Noria Park to let her know that the FBI took him into custody.

"Are you sure?"

"Yes, Ms. Park. They put handcuffs on him and took him away in a government car."

"They must have been bugging the room. All right. I'll take care of it."

Noria makes a call to another one of her North Korean associates.

"Kwon. Lisa Appleton has to be silenced. Do it before she speaks to the police and makes a deal."

"Understood Ms. Park. We'll take care of it."

With that, Noria hoped to tie off any connections between her and Appleton. She realized that working with a civilian was just too risky, so she would not jeopardize the operation like that again. And as for Jan Sawyer, Noria had been contacting her with encrypted emails, like a burner phone, nearly impossible to trace. She paid Sawyer to plant misleading messages on the computers. Anything Sawyer might say would incriminate her without proof of anyone else being involved.

And fortunately, Eisenberg never met Park; he could only point to Appleton. Any deal he might want to make giving up Appleton would be worthless once she was eliminated. Soon, Noria will have control of the situation, but she would need another way to get information out of 7HTG.

Chapter 10

Captain Williams calls Mariani into her office.

"Tony, the FBI wants you to arrest Lisa Appleton and bring her here. Agent Moore will pick her up later today after she completes the legal paperwork, but here is your warrant, signed by a FISA judge."

"Espionage. I don't think I've ever arrested someone for that. Are you sure we have the authority to serve this?"

"We do. In our capacity helping the FBI, we are authorized to make arrests when we get these warrants. Just pick her up and get right back. You and Dr. Lee have to get up to Seattle to testify in Tamara Yonnua's murder trial." *

from my novel "The Da Vinci Diamond"

"All right. I'll take Officer Johnson."

Mariani finds Johnson and tells her where they are going. "Pam, better wear a vest with SFPD markings. I don't want there to be any misunderstanding about our visit to Miss Appleton."

"Of course detective. I'll be outside in just a minute."

Mariani and Johnson pull up to Lisa Appleton's condo, walk up to the door and ring the bell, while Mariani holds the warrant in his left hand. Appleton opens the door, barefoot and dressed in jeans and a pink sweater. She is shocked to see that Mariani and Johnson, the couple they had met at Scoma's, were really police officers.

"Lisa Appleton, please step outside. You are under arrest on suspicion of espionage, federal statute 139B."

"May I get my purse and shoes detective?" she said as her eyes started to look down, realizing she had been caught.

"Quickly. Officer Johnson, please accompany Ms. Appleton." Johnson walks into the condo and comes out a minute later. She puts handcuffs on Appleton and leads her out the door to their unmarked car.

Suddenly, a loud explosion goes off and Appleton is lying on the ground, a bullet dead center of her chest. Johnson and Mariani pull out their guns. Johnson ducks down while Mariani calls on his radio.

"This is Mariani. Shots fired at our location. The prisoner has been hit. Send a bus and backup immediately."

They quickly pull Appleton back into her condo and shut the door. Mariani checks her pulse and applies pressure to the gunshot wound. Appleton looks at Johnson and grimaces as her life slips away.

Within minutes another police car and an ambulance are on the scene, but it's too late to save Appleton. Mariani directs the cops to search for the evidence the assassin may have left, footprints, a shell casing, but they don't find any.

"Are you all right Pam?"

"Yes detective, just a little scared. I've never been that close to getting shot."

"Let's hope you never do Pam." Mariani felt an extra sense of relief for his partner and lover, realizing he would have to protect her on the job.

Mariani and Johnson return to SFPD.

Chapter 11

Captain Williams meets Mariani and Johnson at the door.

"Are you two all right?"

Mariani speaks first. "Just a close call captain. Johnson was leading Appleton out to our car when the shot was fired."

"Are you OK, Pam?"

"Yes captain. Just a little scared."

"That's what you're supposed to feel. Would worry if you weren't. Well, you'll have some time to recover, but the detective and Dr. Lee have to go to Seattle for Tamara Yonnua's trial."

"All right" said Mariani. "Did they arrange for transportation and hotel?"

"Yes, here are your tickets. If for any reason you're not finished by Friday, then let me know. Otherwise, we'll see you next Monday."

"Will do Captain." Mariani looked at the tickets. "Flight leaves tonight at 6:00pm. David, how about I pick you up at four?"

"Good. See you then."

"Pam, call Agent Moore and let her know that Appleton has been killed. Then update your notes and keep up our surveillance on Jan Sawyer."

"Yes detective. Have a safe trip."

Chapter 12

Noria realized that she would have to find another way to get Intel out of 7HTG. The North Korean engineers had been experimenting with a nano technology listening device. It was virtually impossible to detect, the size of a pinhead, with stealth coating. Noria placed it under the first layer of Sander's jacket, around his shoulder and just behind his collar. You wouldn't be able to see it, even if you knew where to look. The bug, nicknamed MA001 (for miniature audio, first generation), picked up audio from a radius of 10 feet, saved it and sent it to an encrypted internet site, once the device left the top secret environment of the Dutch Windmill. These bugs disintegrated within 48 hours, leaving no trace of their existence, so Noria had to plant them every other day on the clothing that Sanders wore. Since she often picked out his outfits, Noria knew exactly where to set it.

This wasn't traditional intelligence work where people turn assets into information, as Lisa Appleton was doing with Ted Eisenberg, but it was relatively safer, without the complications of morality or the vagaries of the human condition. It was pure technology; the state of the art in espionage and North Korea was on the leading edge of it. The Americans and British also had similar devices, but were using them in the Middle East, where intelligence can mean saving lives.

Chapter 13

Penetrating 7HTG for drone technology was just the first part of the mission Noria Park and the North Korean government had planned. If she could intercept drone programming and send them against U.S. targets, she would have to make it look like another country had done so. They were planning on implicating China, by leaving false evidence tying the drone strikes to Chinese dissidents. They knew that if the U.S. found out that North Korea was behind this, the United States military would launch a severe attack on North Korea with missiles and perhaps nuclear weapons. So secrecy about the mission was paramount.

Their plan to drive a wedge between the United States and China was just beginning. An end to their cooperation would mean North Korea could eventually fulfill their goal of attacking the South and reunifying the country under a communist regime.

Noria Park, as the point person in the United States for the operation, reported only to the highest authorities in North Korea, who gave her all the resources she would need in the operation.

Chapter 14

In a small, but well lit room inside the San Francisco FBI building, Agent Jenny Moore is interrogating Ted Eisenberg.

"Mr. Eisenberg, before we send you off to federal prison, we have some questions."

"I don't know anything. Really!"

"So you don't know Lisa Appleton?"

"Well, yes of course. We were dating."

"I thought you were dating Jan Sawyer."

"How do you know that?" Eisenberg realizes the question was moot. "Just once and a while. We knew each other from college. She got me the interview at 7HTG."

"And are you working with Ms. Sawyer to steal national security information?"

"Wait. No one is stealing information. Jan and I have the same security clearance, the same access to information. Why would you say we're stealing information?"

"Who is behind the disinformation messages popping up on 7HTG computers? Were you planting those messages to distract others from your real mission?"

"Mission? What mission? I don't know anything about those messages. And what do you mean by mission?"

"Passing sensitive and classified information on to undermine our intelligence and military operations."

"Whoa. Why would you say that?"

"Do you know what Lisa Appleton does for a living?"

"She does something in public relations. I'm not sure what."

"She runs an upscale prostitution business in San Francisco."

Eisenberg's face falls flat. He pauses in thought. "I can't believe that."

Agent Moore holds up Appleton's picture. "Did you really think a woman like this would date you? Seriously? She was using you to get intelligence information about your company, well the company you used to work for."

Eisenberg recognizes the delusion he has been under, but still didn't believe he did anything wrong. "I didn't give her any classified information. All we did was personal."

Moore plays the tape back for Eisenberg, reminding him that he told her about drone technology being used in Asia. "Would you care to revise your statement, Mr. Eisenberg?"

At this point, he realizes that he did leak classified information. "I really don't remember that. Lisa was just interested in my work and I wanted to impress her. You can ask her. Hey you probably have already. What did she say?"

"I'm afraid she was eliminated before we could question her."

"She's dead? Oh, no. This is my fault, isn't it?"

"Your only fault was giving her the information. We just have to find out who she was working for, but of course you don't know, do you?"

"No. If I did, I would tell you."

"Well, until we find the extent of the leak, you're going to be held in federal prison. The charge is espionage. If you're lucky, you may get out some day." Moore turns to leave the room.

"Wait. Agent Moore, I'm not a spy. I had no idea a small detail like that would be such a big deal."

"Think a minute Mr. Eisenberg. Telling your bed partner that drones you work on are being used in Asia is not only a breach in your contract as an NSA employee. It may be just the information our enemies need to locate those drones. Would you like to tell a congressional committee that you're the source of a leak that led to an international incident with countries like China and North Korea?"

Eisenberg collapses on the table in front of him, head down and banging his fists. "I didn't know. I didn't know."

"Well, you do now, don't you?" Agent Moore leaves the room.

Agent Moore still didn't know who was planting those messages on computers at 7HTG. But it was actually Jan Sawyer, who was being paid secretly by Noria Park. Sawyer had no idea who Park was or why she would pay her for pranks. She knew that the company wouldn't be able to trace the messages back to her. But when Eisenberg was arrested and fired, she stopped putting up messages on the computers.

Since Eisenberg was the government's prime suspect, Sawyer figured they would blame him for the messages. She stopped getting payments for her disinformation and was glad for it.

Noria Park could always point the FBI to Sawyer, but that was a card she didn't want to play yet. She would see how far she could get with the bugs on Robert Sanders, now that she had the key information about drone use in Asia.

Agent Moore knew that Jan Sawyer might also be involved, so she brought her in for questioning the next day.

"Ms. Sawyer, what do you know about Ted Eisenberg?"

"Well, we work together, but I heard he was just fired. I don't know why."

"In what way do you work together?"

"We both work at 7HTG, that's all. He encrypts information and I write code."

"Code for what Ms. Sawyer?"

"I'm afraid that's classified, Agent Moore. You would have to ask my boss, Robert Sanders."

"You were dating Mr. Eisenberg, weren't you?"

"Well, yes. Once in a while. We knew each other in college. Why?"

Agent Moore holds up a picture of Lisa Appleton. "Did you know Ted was also seeing this woman?"

Sawyer is shocked, seeing the stunning older woman in this picture. "I can't really believe that."

"Why not?"

"Well, it's obvious. This woman is in her thirties and way out of Ted's league."

"Well, we can agree about that. Do you know this woman?"

"No, should I?"

"Perhaps. One more question Ms. Sawyer."

"Yes?"

"Were you sending messages to computers at 7HTG about your classified work, any mention of classified operation code names?"

Sawyer was prepared for this question. She had anticipated how to react. "No, sorry. Was Ted doing that? The messages stopped since he left the company."

"We know. We suspect he may have been doing that too."

"Too? What was he doing? Why was he fired?"

"I'm afraid that is also classified, my dear. That's all for now. You may leave."

"So you only wanted to question me because Ted and I dated?"

"That's about it. Should you be a suspect for anything else?" Moore looked directly into Sawyer's eyes.

"No. Like I said, I'm just a programmer." Sawyer walked out of the room, trying not to show her anxiety.

She knew that Ted must have done something big to have the FBI involved. She walked out of the FBI building, determined to walk the straight and narrow from then on. She was concerned that she might still get caught for planting the misinformation on the computers at 7HTG. But what could she do?

If she knew that Noria Park was a terrorist, she would have never gotten involved. But no one knew the multi-layered attack to come, that is except Noria Park and a select few at North Korea's SSD.

Chapter 15

The next week, Mariani was reviewing Ted Eisenberg's file with Dr. Lee.

"David, it's amazing that Eisenberg gave that information to Appleton, don't you think?"

"He was under the influence Tony. Don't you remember your first hot girl?"

"Ah. Yes. That was Beth. I was lucky enough to keep her, for a while anyway. But I was smart enough not to talk about police business."

"That's because she wasn't a spy and she probably would have stopped you if you did. Beth was a teacher, remember?"

"What does that have to do with it?"

"Well, would you like to hear all the gossip and such that teachers have to deal with, not to mention the nonsense her students probably did on a daily basis?"

"No, guess not."

"Well, she didn't want to hear about murder cases. She just wanted your life together to be about you, not about your cases."

"That's probably why we were so happy together."

"Yes. I think so."

Then a call came over the speaker.

We have an emergency at the BART system. Several of the trains have just stopped. Requesting all officers to the main room immediately for assignment.

"Have to go David." Mariani heads upstairs to with the other officers. Captain Williams is addressing everyone.

"We have a report that several BART trains just stopped. They don't know what's wrong but are asking for our help to control the public. Your assignment is on the board. Call in with any information."

Mariani notices that he and Johnson are assigned to the BART control center. He sees Johnson and waves her over. "C'mon Pam. We're on the same assignment."

They drive over to the BART control center and are met by the official in charge, John Rivera. Mariani shows him his credential.

"Mr. Rivera, I'm Detective Mariani and this is Officer Johnson. What's going on?"

"I wish I knew detective. All we know is that four BART trains stopped for no reason. The car men can't get them going. It's unlikely that a mechanical problem caused them all to stop. We're looking at the computer controls now."

"Our other officers are deployed at the stations where those trains stopped, to help with the crowd and prevent panicking."

"That's good. Wait. Here's my software engineer now, Linda Ito. What's going on Linda?"

"Sir. It looks like someone hacked into our system and stopped those trains. There's a timer on the code line. It should release them back to our control within the hour."

"Can you tell who did this?" said Mariani.

"No sir. There isn't any signature or way to trace it back. They went in, planted the code and got out, probably so we couldn't trace the intrusion."

"And you say the code will release the trains within the hour?"

"Yes, it appears so. I have to meet with the security team to see if we can find out how they got in."

John Rivera nods. "Go ahead Linda. Thanks. Let me know the moment you find something and what we're going to do to prevent this from happening again."

Mariani takes some notes. "Mr. Rivera, I think you should make a statement to the media that this was just a computer error, but not mention anything else."

"Of course. Our public information officer will make a statement."

"Don't make it sound critical. We don't want the people who did this to think they were able to have a major impact on the public."

"Yes, you're right. We will contact you when we get more details. The trains should be back on schedule at eleven o'clock. I'm just glad this didn't happen at rush hour this morning."

"Good. I'm going to have one of our tech officers talk with Ms. Ito. She can fill him in on any details, any place we can start looking for a suspect."

"Here's my card. Have the tech call me and I'll get them together. Thanks for your quick response detective."

"You're welcome sir. Let's hope we can prevent this from happening again."

Mariani and Johnson go back to the precinct. They give Captain Williams the information. The officers in the field are notified that they are to treat this as a minor incident and wait for the trains to start moving again at eleven o'clock, which they did.

Captain Williams isn't about to take the situation lightly. She closes the door with Tony while Johnson and others wait outside.

"Tony, stopping four trains for an hour is one thing. What if those trains were directed to drive toward each other? We would have a major accident, a terrorist act."

"I'm concerned too captain. We need to find who is behind this before they take the next step. This looks like a trial run, to see if they could get into the system. We'll need to have BART find the hole in security, but in the meantime, our tech team will work with them to investigate."

"Good. Until then, why don't you keep the details on a need to know basis. And let Johnson and the tech team know not to tell any others either."

"Of course captain."

Chapter 16

San Francisco is a very expensive city to live in. When Pam moved from the East coast, she could only afford a room in the house of a Chinese family outside of North Beach, the Italian section of the city. She spent one or two nights a week at Tony's condo and every weekend. Fortunately for her, she had regular hours, eight to five, Monday to Friday and weekends off. Normally, rookie officers would have to work night shifts and weekends, but as Tony's partner, she inherited his senior detective work schedule.

So they usually ended their day at 5pm. This Thursday, Captain Williams wanted to keep all the detectives after work to discuss the situation at BART, to create a strategy for them to find the hacker and to heighten their vigilance in case this was the beginning of a more serious terrorist threat.

Pam told Tony she would meet him at home for dinner while he stayed late for the meeting. She stopped by Rosa's grill in North Beach to pick up dinner and cannoli. Pam was very comfortable living with Tony. She began to put some feminine touches into the condo with her clothing and personal items. She brightened up the space with colored pillows and drapes, but it all worked for Tony, who hadn't had a woman in his life since his wife died a couple years ago.

When Tony got in around 7pm, his lovely partner greeted him, barefoot and wearing a light brown peasant dress. Red candles lit the small dining table and the scent of Italian food was in the air.

Tony smiled, and then took off his jacket and tie. Pam met him and put her arms around his neck. As she pressed her body against his, they kissed for a minute. When she leaned back, he pulled her close for another kiss.

"What a wonderful way to end the day. What are we eating?"

"Rosa prepared two chicken picatta dinners, salad and cannoli. I also picked up some Italian bread and warmed it up. You like?"

Tony rubbed Pam's back, and then held out her chair. Taking his seat, he now seemed very relaxed, almost forgetting the stressful job he had. "Everything is perfect dear."

Pam poured two glasses of Chianti. They toasted each other, ate dinner and headed to the bedroom. A glorious hour later, they emerged to have their cannoli and tea. Pam preferred tea, so Tony was trying to switch from coffee.

"How about a walk dear? I'd like some fresh air."

"Sure, let me show you some place that was special to me when I was a child."

They walked across Washington Square past Saints Peter and Paul Church, the white spires lighted at night.

"This is where I go to mass Pam. I was an altar boy here."

"I'm afraid I'm a lapsed Catholic Tony. Haven't gone regularly for quite some time now."

"That's OK. Maybe you can try this out sometime."

"I'd like that. I really should get back to mass and confessional."

"Confessional?"

"Yes dear, don't you think?"

"We're all sinners Pam, but you are pure of heart."

Pam snuggled up into Tony's shoulder. "So are you dear. So are you."

The next morning was Saturday, a day Pam and Tony often spent wandering around the Bay Area. But they couldn't get the BART situation off their mind.

"Let's take a look at the BART map Pam, to see if we can figure out why those four trains were stopped yesterday."

"OK, I'll bring one up on the laptop."

"Plug your laptop into the big screen for a larger picture." Pam sent her picture to Tony's big television; the BART map appeared in full color."

"Hmm. All four of the trains that were stopped were headed to the financial center. A red line train stopped off the stop for Embarcadero, a green line outside Powell Street, a yellow line at Montgomery and a blue line at Civic Center and UN Plaza."

"Looks like that would have caused quite a gridlock if it was done at rush hour."

"Exactly Pam. That's what I was thinking. But there are other critical stops. Both airports, Oakland City Center and Berkeley. If you add those to the financial center closings, you could pretty much shut down San Francisco for a while."

"But why would someone do that?"

"I'm just speculating, but what if a terrorist planted a bomb of some kind and wanted to trap as many people as possible in the area."

"You really think that's possible Tony?"

"I hope not, but it isn't impossible. A lot of federal workers work here too. FBI and other national security offices. San Francisco is actually a prime terrorist target. And don't forget our friends at 7HTG. They are probably not the only group here doing classified work for the government."

"Maybe your imagination is running away with you dear."

"I hope that's all. The authors and movie makers seem to think that Armageddon is just around the corner."

"Do you have to go in today for the BART problem."

"No, but I'm on call if anything else happens. Let's hope that hack into their system has been plugged now."

"If it hasn't, then you'll probably be one of the first to know, huh? Is that what your meeting was about last night?"

"Yes. All the senior detectives in the city have been issued new code words for terrorist activities and are to be on alert for texts calling us in. But you'll probably come in with me if I do, to help investigate."

"Just a few years ago I was in college studying forensic science. Now I'm with you watching for terrorists. Can't believe it."

"You're a good partner Pam, in more ways than one." Tony leaned over to kiss her. "But let's not spend the whole day tomorrow worrying about terrorists. Let's take a walk on the Embarcadero and enjoy the bay."

Chapter 17

Noria Park and Robert Sanders were also spending the day in the city. Leaving their Marina District condo, they walked across the Golden Gate Bridge, stopping to picnic at the Marin County side. While Robert's head was full of romance with his Asian beauty, Noria was watching the city on the other side as the target for her terrorist plan.

"Aren't the sailboats beautiful Bob?"

"Yes. I wish I sailed. Never did learn back at prep school."

"Maybe we could charter a boat and someone to take us sometime."

"Yes. I'd like that too. Around the bay or overnight?"

"Oh. Overnight of course. I want to spend a hot night with you on the water."

"Mmm. I'd like that too Noria." Sanders pulled out his tablet and searched for chartered boats.

Noria loved that about him. In spite of the fact that she was using him to advance her plot, she did have genuine feelings for him.

"Make sure you find one for just a few couples with a private room." She ran her hand down his.

"Of course dear. Here's one that leaves on Friday night and gets back on Sunday night. Goes down to Santa Barbara with a stop at Carmel on Sunday afternoon."

"Sounds perfect dear. Lovemaking and a cruise. Do they show the menu?"

"Here it is." He hands the tablet to Noria.

"Ooh. Seafood, fresh fruit and some nice desserts. And Italian on Saturday night. I'm ready to go."

Sanders was falling in love with Noria. It would have been a perfect romance, except for the whole dating a North Korean terrorist complication. But Noria was quite an expert at hiding her true identity, so he didn't have any clue about the disaster to come.

Chapter 18

Noria was ready to put the next step into action. Her tech team had managed to take the code Eisenberg was working on and rewrite it to intercept U.S. Drones in Asia, particularly in Pakistan. Now it was time to test their ability to direct those drones.

The plan was to intercept a drone in Pakistan and send it to Tashgurgan, a remote and ruined city in China, fly around a bit, take photos and return to Shamsi Airfield, a base in Pakistan used for covert operations. The Chinese would undoubtedly see the drone in their airspace and investigate.

The SSD kept this plan secret, not even telling the Chinese Ministry of State Security (MSS). The Chinese knew that the U.S. had plans for sending drones into China; they just didn't think it would happen this soon.

The Chinese military attempted to shoot down the drone but didn't reach the remote village soon enough. Local police did take some video of it and sent it to the MSS.

When the American military inspected the drone, they found the video of Tashgurgan and notified their superiors who contacted the pentagon in Washington, D.C. Within hours, there was a meeting of military and intelligence officials.

"What was it doing in China?" said the head of drone operations for the military to the CIA operative for Pakistan.

"We don't know sir. We didn't send it into China. The drone must have been hacked."

"Hacked! And who is responsible for protecting that from happening?"

"There are contractors who work for the NSA in San Francisco. They encrypt all of the programming in the drones to prevent hacking."

"Well, I think someone is going to answer for this. We don't send drones into China for any reason, much less a trial surveillance mission."

"Yes sir. I'll get them on the phone at once."

"You better get their ass here at once. I want to talk to the head of that group personally."

"Yes sir. Robert Sanders from the 7 Hills Technology Group. I'll get him here immediately."

Meanwhile, diplomatic efforts were attempting to keep the incident from escalating. The state department had orders to convey our regret for the intrusion. The President even sent a secret communiqué stating that we have no intentions of violating China's air space for such a mission. Both militaries were put on alert. One little drone had increased the tensions of the world's two super powers, almost directing them to hostilities.

The next day Robert Sanders was at the Pentagon, meeting with military and intelligence officials.

"So Mr. Sanders, you think the programming for this drone was hacked and sent to China. Do you have proof of this?"

"Yes sir. The code was sent back to our office in San Francisco. Our engineers determined that the code was changed to make that flyover in Tashgurgan. We don't know who did it or why."

"You may not know Mr. Sanders, but I can guess why. Some terrorist might just want to start a war between the United States and China. Does that sound feasible to you?"

"Yes sir. That might be an eventual outcome."

"Well, until you secure your code Mr. Sanders, we're grounding all drones in Pakistan."

"Yes sir."

"Are you sure this couldn't be one of your employees?"

"Oh, not possible sir. Why do you ask?"

"Well, I have this report that one of your engineers, a Ted Eisenberg, was arrested by the FBI for leaking classified information."

Sanders was turning red from the interrogation. "Yes sir. But he was immediately taken out and has been in FBI custody, unable to communicate with anyone."

"I also see that he was dating someone named Lisa Appleton. Perhaps he passed information along to her."

"Miss Appleton was assassinated the day after Eisenberg was caught. It's unlikely she even saw any code at all."

"But it's not impossible either, is it Mr. Sanders?"

"We immediately changed all the encryption on the drone technology, as soon as Eisenberg was removed."

"Well Mr. Sanders, you better tighten up that encryption or you're not going to working for the NSA anymore. Do you understand?"

"Completely General. We have the utmost loyalty to the United States and to our mission. We don't think you will find any more drones going off target."

"We better not Mr. Sanders. I suggest you get back to San Francisco."

"Yes sir."

Sanders delivered the bad news to his staff personally, in the SCIF, in order to maintain security on the subject. All programming codes for the drones were re-encrypted, with a second layer of encryption on top of that. The drones would be impervious to hacking. A self-destruct mechanism was to be added to ensure even if an enemy captured a drone, the software and hard disk would be burned up.

But Noria and her engineers already had what they wanted, basic flight and navigational code to direct their own drone, within the United States.

Chapter 19

As a follow up to security at 7HTG, FBI Agent Jenny Moore was notified about the drone mishap. She was to oversee Robert Sanders and the code corrections made for national security.

They met in 7HTG's secure SCIF room.

"So Mr. Sanders. I understand you had quite a grilling at the Pentagon."

"Yes ma'am. Nothing I want to experience again."

"Are your engineers confident that we have eliminated the problem?"

"As sure as possible Agent Moore. Two layers of the highest level of encryption possible with a self destruct mechanism being added in case a drone is ever captured by our enemies."

"Well, that sounds good. I know how well your group is considered in D.C. I would hate to think that all the good work you did would end because of one incident."

"We're taking this as seriously as possible."

"Do you think Mr. Eisenberg had anything to do with it?"

"We don't think so. The code is so massive; it can't easily be copied and taken out of the building. He may have said some inappropriate things to Lisa Appleton in order to bed her, but it is virtually impossible for him to pass sensitive code to her."

"Let's hope so. Is it possible that the navigational system just failed?"

"No, it was hacked. We saw how the code was changed."

"Could Mr. Eisenberg have done it?"

"Yes, but it would have still been a one in a thousand chance that anything he did could get to operational missions in Pakistan. There's just too many fail safes."

"Fail is the word they don't like sir."

"Yes, ma'am. It won't happen again."

"Thank you Mr. Sanders. I hope you're right."

But Sanders had one of those nano bugs on his jacket that Noria planted, so she heard the entire conversation. This confirmed that their efforts to intercept a U.S. drone have succeeded. Even if 7HTG made the drones impenetrable from then on, their theft of basic navigation code was important for her planned terrorist attack.

Chapter 20

Noria Park's plan to have Lisa Appleton get sensitive Intel from Ted Eisenberg may have failed, but she had several other female agents under her direction for the master plan. As she did with Appleton, Park recruited women from several other ethnic backgrounds, to further distance the operation from North Korea.

There was Maria Ruiz, a fiery Latina woman. U.S. Border patrol agents crossed over into Mexico illegally and killed Ruiz's brother. North Korean agents found her on Internet sites sympathetic to anti-government rhetoric.

And Sonya Niguel, an Indian by birth, involved with gathering intelligence on nuclear weapons in South Asia. Sonya's interest in terrorism stemmed from being rebuffed for government positions in New Delhi.

Finally, there was Susan Kate, who was the All-American girl. Blonde hair, blue eyes and preppy clothing. That's why she was so effective as a spy, blending into corporations as a temp worker or contractor. Her specialty was stealing industrial secrets for competitors, but her darker past drove her to Park's team.

All three were masters at seduction, technology and manipulation. They would play a key role in the attack on the U.S. However, none of them had met Park, not yet. She gave her instructions through encrypted texts and emails. They only knew her as 'the butterfly' a name Park got from a North Korean General who she did some spying for. She left him as soon as the job was over, flitting back to North Korean's secret intelligence agency, the State Security Department or SSD.

The SSD provided other resources for Park, especially technology expertise. High-level programmers who could write code to send drones to targets, like Eisenberg did, only working a terrorist agenda. These programmers were in both North Korea and the United States, and several were trained at elite universities here, like MIT and Cal Tech.

Chapter 21

In the Korean section of San Francisco, a call came in to the precinct. A murder. Captain Williams sent Mariani, Johnson and David Lee to the scene. Local cops marked off the crime scene, a Korean grocery on Telegraph Avenue. Mariani questioned the officer on the scene.

"What do we have officer?"

"Looks like a robbery detective. The owner's daughter saw a man shoot her father after demanding money from the register. He gave them everything in the register, but was shot anyway."

"Do you have a time?"

"Yes. Two-thirty five. The daughter was in the store when it happened."

"Is that his daughter?" said Mariani, pointing to the girl crying in the corner.

"Yes sir. Alice Kwan. She's nineteen years old."

"David, why don't you start on the body while Pam and I talk to the daughter."

"Yes, Tony."

"Miss Kwan. My name is Detective Mariani; this is Officer Johnson. I'm very sorry for your loss."

The daughter took a minute to compose herself, and then answered while sobbing. "He didn't have to do it. My father gave him the money. Why did he kill him?"

"Sometimes there isn't an answer. But we will do our best to find the person who did this. Can you describe the man who robbed the store?"

"He had a wool cap on and gloves, but I could tell he was a white man. He was short, maybe five feet six inches and he shot my father with a pistol."

"That's good. Was there anyone else in the store when this happened?"

"Just a couple of regular customers. When they saw the gun, they ran out."

"Are you sure they were customers you knew?"

"Yes. They are from the neighborhood."

"Are there any security cameras?"

"Oh. I forgot. Yes, we do have one. It records from that camera." She pointed to a camera positioned behind the register where customers would pay. "It feeds onto a website. I can give you the address of our security company."

"That's very helpful Alice. May I call you Alice?"

"Yes, actually that helps. I'm feeling very scared right now."

"Of course. Is it just you and your father in the store?"

"My mother passed away last year, but I have a brother, Jim. He's in college at Cal. Oh no. How will I tell him?"

"Why don't you call him? Officer Johnson, would you stay with Alice while she finds her brother?" Mariani gave Johnson a look, indicating she should take the daughter away from the body.

"Yes detective. Alice, let's go in the back and call Jim."

Mariani went over to Dr. Lee. "Well David. What do you have?"

"Just like you can imagine. One gunshot to the center of the chest at close range. It's a shame his daughter had to witness this."

"Yes. Pam is with her now. She's calling her brother. So nothing else remarkable about the body?"

"I'll know after the autopsy. But unless I find another bullet hole, that's the cause of death."

"His daughter told the officer on the scene that there was only one shot. All right, let's get him out of here so we can start to help his daughter recover. I want this cleaned up as soon as we finish taking pictures. No need to leave this mess here overnight."

"Of course. Was there security video from that camera?"

"Yes, it fed directly to a security company. Pam and I will go over there after we see the brother; you can take the body back."

"Yes Tony. We can get this done right away."

Mariani went to the back office to see how the daughter was doing. "Alice, were you able to contact Jim?"

"Yes. He's coming in now. He should be here in a half hour."

"We will stay with you."

"Thank you."

"Of course. Is this monitor part of the security system?"

"Yes. You can watch the video her by controlling that dial. Let me rewind it to the time before the robbery."

"Are you sure you can do that Alice?" Mariani didn't want her to relive the moment her father was killed.

"Maybe you're right."

"Officer Johnson. Take Alice outside and put her in a patrol car until her brother comes in. I want to question him about who might have done this."

"Yes detective."

Mariani looked over the security video feed and rewound it back to the time of the robbery. He could confirm Alice's account of the robber's height and ethnicity. But his trained eye could see more than Alice could. He saw a small tattoo on one arm, a gang tattoo. He also noticed someone waiting outside the grocery to pick the robber up. He identified the car as a late model black pick up truck, maybe a Toyota. With these details, he was able to call in an update to the initial patrolman's report. After he finished updating the report to the precinct, Johnson came in the office.

"I thought you were staying with Alice."

"I am, but she told me something important. She says that her father always kept several trace bills in the register, in case they were robbed."

"Trace bills?"

"Yes, apparently they have a micro wire inserted into the paper and they emit a GPS signal. She gave me the details here."

"Never heard of this before. Do you know how to track the bills?"

"Using this information, I can. Let me sit at the computer."

Pam Johnson went to the website listed and input the identifying numbers associated with the trace bills. Within thirty seconds, a map of the city with a beeping orange dot appeared on her screen.

"There's the money, on the corner of 16th and Mission. The dot isn't moving so they have stopped there."

"Great. I'll call it in to a local patrol car. We need to get more information about these tracer bills. They could be really useful in undercover operations, especially for our colleagues in narcotics and vice."

"I'll take care of it Tony. I have the details on the system for tracking the bills; we should be able to find out who creates them."

Mariani called a local unit to the scene, with a description of the robber and truck. Within the hour, they had them in custody and recovered the money. Mariani and Johnson were consoling Alice and Jim Kwan when they got the call.

"Again we are so sorry for your loss. But I have some good news. We have arrested the man who robbed the store and killed your father. With your description and these surveillance video, we should be able to convict him."

Alice and Jim hugged each other, even though this was little consolation. It seemed to Johnson and Mariani that this did lighten their pain a little.

"Thank you detective. This does help." Then she began crying again into her brother's arms.

"We will be in touch soon Alice. Jim. Dr. Lee has made sure that the store was cleaned up. We won't need to be in there anymore."

"So my father's blood is all gone?"

"Yes."

"Oh, thank goodness. I was dreading going in there."

Jim thanked Mariani and Johnson as they returned to the grocery, now a painful reminder of the worst day of their lives.

Mariani and Johnson rode back to the precinct.

"Good work back there Pam." Mariani noticed that Pam was crying. "Are you all right?"

"Yes. I just feel so bad for those kids, losing their father that way. I guess it's not professional. I'll stop now."

Mariani squeezed her hand. "Never be sorry for feeling badly. I'm sure Alice knew that you cared. It is one of the most important qualities an officer can have."

"Thanks Tony."

Chapter 22

The next test for Park and her team was to disperse a poison gas through a mini drone shaped like a butterfly. Her underling, Sonya Niguel planted the harmless looking creature on top of a bed of flowers in Golden Gate Park, and then watched from a safe distance as tourists wandered through.

A family walked by first, the wife and daughter pausing long enough to take a picture of the butterfly flapping its wings a few feet out of their reach. Sonya controlled the deadly insect with commands from an app on her phone, sending the butterfly darting in and out of the flowers. She was given strict orders not to kill any children, so she waited until the family had moved along.

Next came a young man and woman walking hand in hand. The boy listened intently to his girlfriend as she described her dreams to him. Then she noticed the butterfly popping around the flowers. As lifelike and realistic as could be, these spy craft drones were meant to blend into nature, like the walking stick directional microphone and the surveillance hummingbird. The girl held out her palm to entice the red and black, four-inch insect to land there, but Sonya pulled it out of her reach and view just in time. They walked by, not realizing how close they came to the end of their love story.

But here was a homeless man, with dirty army fatigues, a backpack and a shopping cart, pushing his way to his homestead on the less traveled part of the park. He pulled out a plastic bottle of water to drink. Sonya guided the butterfly gently to land on it. Quietly startled, the vagrant pulled the water bottle away from his face. The butterfly sprayed a small amount of white gas into his eyes, and then floated away. The man cursed the bug, wiped his eyes with his sleeve and walked away. Within a minute, however, he fell to the ground, silently and permanently. No screaming, no clutching of his chest, just the sound of his body dropping dead.

On their way back to the car, the young couple saw the man and called 911. A short time later a patrol officer was on the scene, checked that he was dead and reported it to Mariani's precinct. Twenty minutes later, Mariani and Dr. Lee were on the scene.

"I don't know detective. The caller said he just lay there. I checked for blood and signs of disturbance but didn't see any."

"All right officer. Let's see what the good doctor says."

Dr. Lee examined the body, looking for an obvious cause of death. "I'm going to need to take this one back to autopsy before I can tell you what happened. But the patrolman is right. There are no obvious signs or a gunshot or stab wound, or even a blow to the head. He just seems to have collapsed."

"All right doctor. Let's get him back. Officer Cirillo, we'll take it from here; thanks for giving us a call on this one."

"I was afraid I might be wasting your time."

"Better that than to miss a murder victim. Especially with such a curious circumstance as this."

"Thank you sir."

Dr. Lee and Mariani brought the body back to Lee's autopsy room and he began his examination.

"David, I'll be upstairs starting the paperwork on this one. Give me a call when you have something."

"Will do Tony."

An hour later, Mariani got a text from Lee, requesting his presence downstairs.

"Do you have a cause of death David?"

"I do Tony, but you're not going to believe it."

"Try me."

"This man was poisoned by a very toxic gas, a derivative of cyanide but much more concentrated. I only found a small trace of it in his nostrils and lungs."

"Who would go to such extremes on a homeless man in the park?"

"That's what I thought. I'll write this up and send it to you."

"I'm not sure what else we can do. A homeless man in the park poisoned. Maybe someone obsessed with ridding the park of these vets. The sophistication of the kill bothers me. The killer could have used more conventional weapons, but this was quiet, maybe a test for some future killing on a larger scale. Do you think we would find any trace of this poison in the park?"

"I doubt it Tony. Like I said, the amount in his system was barely noticeable and if there was any quantity in the air, we would be seeing more bodies dropping. Just to be sure though, I'll take a tech with me and go back there to collect air samples."

"All right. Let me know either way."

Tony went back upstairs to his office where Officer Pam Johnson was waiting.

"Sorry I missed the call detective. Captain had me doing some work in the evidence room."

"Actually, I'm glad you weren't there. Dr. Lee and I found a homeless man who collapsed in the park. It turns out the man was poisoned by a very toxic gas."

"Who would go to such lengths to kill a homeless man in the park?"

"Who indeed Pam? It could be a serial killer obsessed with the homeless or something even more sinister."

"Terrorists?"

"It's a possibility. This could have been a test run using the gas. Either way, we have to keep the file open on this one and watch for any related incidents. Why don't you search our computer files for the last five years and see what you can find. Any poisonings or attacks on the homeless. Maybe there's a connection."

"Right away Tony."

As Pam left to research her computer, Tony wondered if this might be connected to the BART train incident. If someone was planning on stopping trains and dispersing a poison gas, that certainly would be terrorism.

Chapter 23

Noria Park's plan included more high tech attacks. She delivered a drone shaped like a seagull to Susan Kate; the mission was to fly it into a water supply with a biological agent.

She released the seagull not far from 7HTG's secret location under the North Church windmill, into the ocean just off The Cliff House, a popular restaurant high above the Pacific Ocean.

Some sea lions washed on shore the next day. Animal control came to retrieve them. As part of their normal cause of death investigation, the unit discovered that a chemical that could have been found naturally in the ocean had poisoned them. Releasing the information to the local papers, the report caught the eye of Pam Johnson who was in charge of monitoring the media for any suspicious news. She brought the article in to the precinct and showed it to Mariani.

"Detective. Look at this. Three sea lions washed up on shore. The animal control unit determined they died of a chemical poison. Do we have any industries that might be dumping in that area?"

"Hmm. Saxitoxin. This wouldn't come from any company. This is a biological agent, used in the military."

"The report says that saxitoxin is a paralytic found in shellfish. Couldn't the sea lions have ingested crabs and died?"

"Look at the concentration Pam. This is a hundred times the normal amount found in shellfish. And the breakdown shows that it isn't the natural form found in shellfish; it has a stabilizer in it. That proves it was man made."

"So why would anyone want to kill marine life?"

"Not marine life Pam. This is biological warfare, perhaps a test to see if someone can put it in a water supply reservoir. Notify homeland security and Agent Moore please."

"Right away detective."

Chapter 24

Within the hour, Agent Jenny Moore was at the precinct, meeting with Mariani and his team. Captain Williams had them meet in her office.

"It's starting to look like terrorist activity," said Captain Williams to Agent Moore." She pointed to the white board connecting the recent events.

"We had a homeless man poisoned by a neurotoxin in the park. Now we have marine life killed by a biological agent, Saxitoxin. Add this to the shutdown of BART trains earlier this month and we have reasonable facts to link this to terrorism."

"How was the poison gas and saxitoxin delivered to the targets?"

"We don't know. The ocean is too big to watch with surveillance cameras and we don't even know when the toxin was put there. Same with the park, although the small dose of gas that killed the homeless man had to be delivered in close quarters because there wasn't any trace of it when we took readings there."

"So the perpetrators are hitting soft targets with no surveillance cameras. That's about as difficult to stop as it comes. Captain, we'll put out an alert to the entire city to be aware of these locations. Maybe police presence will make them step back."

"Maybe at BART stations, but they're unlikely to hit the park and ocean again. I'll tell my precinct to think outside the box. If this is about a terrorist attack to come, it will certainly be directed to larger populations."

"That's what worries me. Have there been any incidents outside the city?"

"Not that we're aware of. We'll send out this scenario to all major cities in the U.S., just in case San Francisco is the testing ground, but the real target is somewhere else."

Mariani is concerned about coordinating all these agency intelligence groups. "How can we keep all this Intel contained and disseminated?"

The agent from homeland security responded. "Good question detective. We'll assign a code name for all possible terrorist threats to San Francisco. How about *Operation Seven Hills*? I understand you're aware of our NSA contractor here The Seven Hills Technology Group."

"Yes sir. In fact, that's just about what I was going to tell you. We had been brought in to investigate a possible breach of their security, but we caught the person responsible, a Ted Eisenberg. Apparently, nothing really classified got out and the only person Eisenberg was working with was assassinated."

"Why are you so sure nothing classified was leaked?"

"Well, to be honest, we can't know for sure. We only know that 7HTG reported that the breach into their computers has stopped and they have completed changing their firewalls and adding a third layer of encryption."

"That sounds promising. Just to be safe, keep up your conversations with them."

Agent Moore follows up. "We have sir. I am the liaison between them and the SFPD. If anything else happens there, they will let us know."

"All right. The 7HTG incident will be added to the Operation Seven Hills folder. Who is your tech person Captain?"

"Officer Pam Johnson manages the digital information here." Johnson steps forward.

"This could be planning for a terrorist attack. Officer Johnson, we're going to get you access to the homeland security alerts and set you up as the SFPD liaison here for communications."

"Thank you sir."

"You have to start thinking like a terrorist, predicting future outcomes, playing what if with the information."

Captain Williams supports Johnson's position. "She won't be alone. Our senior officers will get to review all the data. And FBI Agent Moore will be part of our analysis team."

"Very well. But let's try to prevent any media attention. Panic is the worst element to add to the situation. Terrorists use panic to drive their agenda. Think of all the subsequent attacks after 911."

Pam Johnson questions. "What attacks sir?"

"Exactly. We stopped at least five attacks because of our Intel, areas where terrorists were taking advantage of New Yorker fears. But we kept the media out of it and set up a net of communication unlike anything ever done inside the U.S."

"So you have a model for us to work from?"

"Yes. We'll send you a manual to work from. Tells you the protocols and communication lines. Also includes security codes. FBI Agent Moore can fill you in."

"Yes sir."

Chapter 25

The last agent in Noria Park's operation was Maria Ruiz, a comely Latina. Her assignment was to launch a small drone with high explosives into the new Bay Bridge, at night, disrupting the light show and into one of the suspect bolts that caused such a delay in building. This drone was shaped like a large black crow, almost invisible at night. The crow would explode and disintegrate leaving no clue behind as to the source of the attack.

But first, Ruiz had to test the explosive on a similar structure. The old Bay Bridge, scheduled to be taken down over the next few years, provided a perfect opportunity.

She launched the crow at night to conceal her work. The crow glided around the bay and landed, as targeted, on a section of the old bridge where three metal girders were joined. The explosion was small but intense. First a fire burned off the bolts and then a large section of the bridge fell into the bay. The crow incinerated too, falling in tiny pieces into the water below. Ruiz observed the entire explosion from a waterfront restaurant, north of the ballpark.

As she smiled at her accomplishment, a man came by. "May I join you?" said the handsome guest.

"Oh." Ruiz was startled but quickly regained her composure. "Certainly. I'm Maria. Maria Ruiz."

The gentleman extended his hand. "Nice to meet you Maria. I'm Mike Dawson. I noticed you were looking out at the bridge. Anything interesting tonight?"

"No. Just cars and stars as usual. I was just daydreaming. Tell me about yourself Mike."

"I'm with the Giants organization. Back office. Statistics and computer work. How about you?"

"Women's clothing. I'm an area rep for some stores here."

"Anything I would have heard of?"

"Afraid not. Nothing sexy or scandalous. Everyday wear, sold in the big stores. Target. J.C. Penny. Sears."

Overlooking Maria's pretty sports outfit, Mike commented. "Well, you certainly look nice. Are these some of your line?"

"Oh this. No, something I bought at Macy's. These are supposed to be part of their European sports outfits. Something you might wear to watch Wimbledon."

"Well, I like the colors. And your sneakers. Very cool pink and blue."

"Thanks. You seem casual too. Orange and black. Giant's colors?"

"Of course. You're not a baseball fan, are you?"

"Sorry. More soccer. I'm from Mexico. And you?"

"Born in L.A. I was a minor league player in their farm system, which is until I injured my knee. But the Giants offered me this office job and I wound up in San Francisco. How long have you been in California?"

"Oh, quite a while. My parents moved here when I was in high school. Then I went to college at San Francisco State for fashion design."

"Nice. So you like the bay area?"

"Except for the cost of living."

"Yeah, I know. Do you live in the city?"

"Close, I have a room with some girls I went to college with in Daly City. What about you?"

"Same here. I bunk with a buddy on the team. He pays most of the rent, so I have a great place not too far from here. The team is on the road half the year and off season, so I have the place to myself then."

"Lucky you. So do all baseball players make a lot of money?"

"Well, he does, about $4,000,000 a year, so he bought the condo we are in. He doesn't need a room mate for paying the mortgage, but likes that I'm here when he isn't to keep an eye on the place."

"Is the team in San Francisco now?"

"Actually, they are still on a road trip, in Boston tonight."

"So you're all alone?" Maria's inflection and pouty face gave Mike the opening he was waiting for.

"Yes, sadly. That's why I'm out. Gets lonely at home."

"Maybe we could go back there and have a drink." Maria slid her hand under his.

"I'd like that. Here, let me pay your bill."

"Thank you. Very kind."

Mike left a $20 bill on the table and led Maria out of the restaurant. His condo was only a short walk from the restaurant. By the time they entered the elevator, he had taken her in his arms and kissed her. The door opened and he took her hand to the condo.

"What a lovely view. You can see the bridge from here," said Maria.

"And the ball park looking this way. A number of the players live here."

"Why is the ball park lit up?"

"The grounds crew must be working. Getting ready for the team's return on Monday. Most of the light will go out, but they leave a rim of light around the top every night. I think it's a landmark marker for air traffic coming in to the area."

"It's beautiful. Maybe we could go to a game sometime." Maria took off her jacket and sat on the couch.

Mike took off his Giant's jacket as well. "So what would you like to drink?"

"I was having sangria at the restaurant, but I don't think you would have that, would you?"

"My room mate is from the Dominican Republic. We always have sangria. I'll make you one with some fresh fruit." Mike went into the adjoining kitchen to fix the drinks.

"Perfect. Do you have some music?"

"Sure. Go over and pick out something you like."

Maria leafed through the CD collection. There was a wide selection from rock to jazz to Latin music. She picked out two romantic CDs; one by Chris Botti and one by Marc Antoine. "I found a couple I like."

Mike came back and took the CDs. "Yes, these are very nice. Maybe one more. Do you like Brian Culbertson?"

"I don't know him. Is he good."

"Yes, like the other two you picked out. Smooth jazz."

Mike put the three CDs into the multi-disc player and set the sound field for the speakers. The sound filled the room as if they were at a club listening live.

"Wow, that's great sound," said Maria.

"Glad you like it. This system cost as much as I make in a month." He took her again to kiss her. "The drinks are almost ready. I'm chilling the glasses."

Maria rubbed her hands on Mike's chest, and then leaned into his body with hers. "Sounds good." She sensed Mike's enthusiasm growing.

"I'll be right back." Mike went into the kitchen and came out with a pitcher of sangria, chilled glasses and two Italian pastries. He set them down on the coffee table in front of the couch and poured a glass for Maria.

"Ooh. Dessert too. You weren't expecting company, were you Mike?" Her question was only half serious.

"Oh no. I picked these up after a team dinner in North Beach." He handed the glass to Maria. She looked very sensuous, in a light red Danskin top. Her breasts filled it nicely and her dark black hair fell softly on top.

"Thank you." She took a sip. "Oh, this is very good." Maria took Mike's hand and pulled him closer to her on the couch. Then she pulled his face down to hers and gave him a long, slow kiss. "Mmm. That's nice. You kiss well Mike."

"I think you deserve the credit Maria," gazing into her eyes and those lovely, full lips.

"Why don't we take our sneakers off?"

Mike obliged by taking Maria's off, and then his. Their soft cotton sports pants were drawing each other to them. Maria lay back on the couch and invited Mike on top of her. Mike slid onto her, pressing his chest on her breasts and kissing her slowly. She could feel his groin straining.

"Oh dear. This is wonderful but shouldn't we get a little more comfortable." Maria pulled down Mike's pants and then her own. She took off her socks and then his. Now, in just the Danskin, Mike saw how perfect Maria's body was. He was in good shape too, working out with the team. She took off his top leaving him in just his underpants.

"Mmm. Lover. You look good," Maria said scanning Mike's athletic build.

Mike focused on Maria's beautiful eyes and face, her long hair; then he saw how her 5'8" body fit well with his. "You are so lovely Maria."

With the glow of the lights outside and the soft music inside, Mike and Maria made love, paused to have the desserts, and then retired to his bedroom for the night.

Chapter 26

The harbor police reported the large piece of metal falling from the old Bay Bridge into the water. The FBI and Mariani got the news. Agent Jenny Moore called Mariani.

"What do you think of the explosion on the old Bay Bridge?"

Mariani thought a moment. "What do they know?"

"Only that a piece of the bridge, the size of a stove fell off into the water. Divers are looking for clues."

"Any witnesses to it?"

"No. It happened on the underside of the old bridge, away from any cameras or where drivers could see it from the new span. But it couldn't have just been an accident. The piece they recovered had burn marks. Someone set an explosive there."

"Looks like another test for our file. So no one was hurt?"

"No, thankfully. They will bring the metal to your precinct later for inspection."

"All right. We'll document this incident and add it to our file. Pam will send the report out to everyone on the task force."

When Mariani's team inspected the metal from the bridge, they noticed the burn marks around the edges. But they also found a couple small black pieces of plastic, shaped like a wedge. Mariani asked Dr. Lee what he thought.

"What do you think these are David?"

"I don't know. I'll need to take a look under the scope, maybe run a fragment through our spectrometer. Give me a bit and come back."

"OK." Mariani and Pam finished the initial notice for the task force. "Pam, let's hold this until we get more info from Dr. Lee."

"All right." Then Mariani and Pam got a text from Lee. "Looks like he has something. They went down to Dr. Lee's forensic lab.

"The metal is definitely from the old bay bridge structure. But these wedges are something else."

"What?"

"They're a high composite polymer, like the kind used in sports equipment, very strong. You see it in professional hockey sticks and tennis rackets. Look at this end here." Lee pointed to the narrow end of the piece. "See the tiny hook. I think this went into some device to control movement."

"I thought this was some sort of small missile launch."

"No, the burn patterns indicate a very small surface area. Perhaps a slow moving drone."

"But this isn't shaped like a drone."

"No. It's shaped more like the wing of a bird. You've heard that there are drones disguised as insects and birds?"

"Yes. So what was this?"

"My best guess is a drone shaped like a black bird. Unfortunately this is all we recovered. The rest of it must have disintegrated on contact with the bridge."

"All right. We'll add your analysis to our report and send it out to the task force. Thanks David."

"Very good Tony. I'll send you my report and pictures for an attachment."

Chapter 27

Jan Sawyer was feeling guilty about posting messages on the 7HTG computers. With the FBI and SFPD investigating the employees, she thought she would be caught sooner or later.

Ted showed Jan how data is encrypted and how to recognize when data is hidden. She used that information to discover a signal, although minimal, coming through the data stream inside the building. Jan kept tracing that signal until she found it coming from her boss, Robert Sanders.

"Boss, I think we have a problem."

"What's that Jan?"

"There's some sort of data signal coming from you."

Sanders was both surprised and upset. "What do you mean?"

Jan used a wand scanner, passing it over Sanders. It stopped at the corner of his jacket shoulder and lapel.

"Take your jacket off please." Sanders put the jacket on the back of a chair and Sawyer continued to scan.

"It's right there." Both of them looked intensely at the spot.

"See it. It's barely the size of a dot."

Sanders tried to pick it up, but it disintegrated in his hand.

"Whoa. What was that?"

"Boss, I think it was recording or transmitting data."

"You mean the sounds of voices?"

"Could be. Guess we'll never know now."

"I don't know how it got there."

"Perhaps you're being followed. Someone at NSA, maybe."

"I don't remember anyone coming near me and this jacket." Just then, he had the sinking feeling that maybe Noria had planted it on his jacket."

"Thank you for finding this Jan. I'm going to look into this, track my steps from home to work for the last few days."

But Sanders was pretty sure Noria had planted the bug. But how could he catch her.

"Jan, I want you to scan me tomorrow."

"Sure. Maybe then we'll know more."

If it was Noria planting the bug, he could tell by wearing a different jacket tomorrow and going directly to work without stopping in town for his morning coffee and pastry. If the bug didn't show up, then maybe Noria was innocent. But he was leaning toward his lover as a spy.

"Let's keep this between us, but bring in Sam Cho. Walk with me."

Sanders and Sawyer went to Sam Cho's office, a secure door between them. Sanders put in the code to enter. Sam turned to greet them.

"Hi boss. What's up?"

"Sam, Jan has discovered some sort of bug that was planted on my jacket. It was small, dark grey and the size of a period." Sanders made a dot on paper to show Sam the size.

"Hmm. That's disconcerting. Where is it?"

"It disintegrated when we tried to handle it. What do you think it was?"

"Well it very well could have been a recording bug, nano technology is very sophisticated today. It could have been a bot looking for data or a transmitter recording voices."

"But this is a secure building. It couldn't have transmitted voice or data."

"Well it could once it left the building."

Sanders realized that if Noria had planted the bug, she would realize it was discovered, once it didn't transmit that day. Then she would have a heads up before the next day. His plan to wear a new jacket wouldn't work, because she wouldn't attempt planting another nano bug the next day.

"All right Sam. Let's keep this between the three of us until I have more info."

"Will do boss. We never met."

Sanders went back to his office and called Agent Moore.

"Agent Moore, this is Robert Sanders."

"Yes sir, how can I help you today?"

"I'd like to request you put surveillance on my girlfriend, Noria Park. There may be a chance she is involved in spying."

"What is your evidence?"

"I can't tell you just yet. We're investigating, but please let me know if you see anything unusual."

"Yes, we can do that. I just have to get a warrant. Does this rise to the level of a FISA investigation?"

"I hope not, but I fear so."

"All right. I'll have her under surveillance by the end of the day."

"Thank you Agent Moore."

But by the time the FBI was ready to watch Park, she had disappeared. Apparently, the sudden disruption in signal pinged the servers tracking the nano bug. They told Park that the bug had been discovered.

She quickly moved out of the condo and left her job to go into hiding; where no one knew. In reality, she was still in San Francisco, hiding out in a North Korean safe house, unknown to U.S. authorities. From there, she could continue to plan the terrorist attack.

When Sanders arrived home, he could tell that she had left. He contacted Agent Moore, but the FBI had not been able to locate her yet. Sanders feared that he was about to lose his government contracts and he may lose his freedom as well.

Chapter 28

Robert Sanders met with FBI Agent Jenny Moore, Detective Mariani, Pam Johnson, Jan Sawyer and Sam Cho at 7HTG.

Sanders led everyone into the SCIF meeting room and closed the door. Then he input the code for security. A line of blue light circumvented (SIC) the top of the wall and a slightly audible low hum began.

"All right everyone. The room is secure now. Jan, why don't you tell us what you found?"

"We found a nano bug planted on Mr. Sanders' jacket. Sam Cho believes that it could have been a recording and transmitting device."

Sam Cho continued. "This is not anyone's fault. We bring it to your attention so that you will be extra careful with what you are wearing or carrying into work. If you have any concerns, let us know and we'll scan the item for technology."

"Have you followed up on the bug?"

Agent Moore responded. "We have an idea of how the bug was planted and we are investigating a possible suspect. That's all we can tell you."

But what Agent Moore wasn't telling them was significant. She felt that this was part of the terrorist attack. She could see how the BART disruption, Bay Bridge explosion, drone poisoning in Golden Gate Park and the chemical agent found in the Pacific Ocean that killed three seals all fit into a conspiracy of something major.

Noria Park was also concerned. Even though she didn't need any more technology from the 7HTG, her cover was blown. She would have to work even more discretely with her field agents to prepare the attack.

Chapter 29

Noria Park's agents had to blend into San Francisco society to avoid suspicion. Susan Kate was getting ready to attend a fundraiser at the San Francisco Symphony.

Kate was dressed in an expensive black gown befitting her place in society. She attended Stanford, majoring in French Literature, a fairly useless major unless your family is wealthy and can provide for your future. It's also good preparation for the Junior League, where Susan was just admitted. Junior League members married the most eligible men, raised perfect families and hosted charity events in their spare time.

But Susan had a rebellious side. She wanted to make a statement before retiring to a life of leisure. So when Noria Park offered her the chance to make her statement, she jumped at it. Today's appearance at the fundraiser was the perfect place to disassociate herself from her mission while playing nice with the wealthy there. She sidled up to a man in a tuxedo at the bar.

"A glass of Chardonnay please."

Turning to face the athletic beauty, the man leaned in. "Let me pay for that dear."

"Why thank you sir. I'm Susan?"

"Lovely to meet you Susan. I'm Joseph. I haven't seen you before."

"Well, I just moved back to town from France. But I went to school here."

"Stanford?"

"Yes. How did you know I didn't go to Cal?"

"I didn't. Just guessed."

"An honest man. I'm impressed."

"And your major was Fine Art."

"Sorry, French Literature. Close enough. What about you?"

"Sports medicine. UCLA. I'm doing a residency in Palo Alto."

"Joseph, where have you been all my life?"

"Susan, I was just about to say that." They laughed.

It was exactly what Noria Park wanted for Susan, to blend in with the social set and establish relationships. Susan met some of Joseph's doctor friends and wives and later let him take her home.

Chapter 30

Jan Sawyer was feeling increasingly guilty about her part in disrupting 7HTG's operations, especially since the gravity of the nano bug meeting. When she found out about the drone misdirected to China, she worried that she might be a suspect, even though she didn't make any changes to the drone technology code.

Robert Sanders called her into his office.

"Jan, I want to make sure you weren't involved in this drone fiasco. Did you have anything to do with redirecting that drone into China?"

Jan's stomach was tense. "No sir. I didn't even know until you debriefed us about it."

"Do you think it was Ted? He seemed to be close with you."

"Well, we dated but I never heard him talk about classified information outside of work."

"You heard about his relationship with that prostitute, yes?"

"Yes, as soon as I did, I lost a lot of respect for him."

"Do you think he posted those messages on our servers, those hacks?"

Jan knew it was now or never. If she confessed, she would certainly be fired. If she didn't admit it and they found out, she could be prosecuted. "I don't know sir. He never mentioned it to me."

"Well, keep your ears open. Someone posted those. If it were internal, that would be bad for our reputation, but if the hacks came from outside, then we would have a much larger security problem."

"Yes sir. I'll let you know."

"Very well Jan. Back to work."

Jan couldn't concentrate for the rest of the day. When she got home, she started drinking. Then she took some sleeping pills, too many pills and never woke up.

The next morning Sanders called FBI Agent Moore and told her that Sawyer didn't come into work. Moore notified Mariani and they met at Sawyer's condo. After knocking several times, Mariani had a tech pick the lock. When they came in, everything was neat and in its place, until they got to the bedroom.

"David, I think Ms. Sawyer may have overdosed."

David Lee inspected the body, saw the alcohol and pills and concurred with Mariani. "Looks that way Tony. We'll know after I examine her stomach contents and do a toxicity screen. Let's get her back to my lab."

Mariani looked around. There were no signs of a struggle or break in. On her high tech desk, next to her computer was a note.

I was the one who posted those messages at work. Someone paid me anonymously to do it. That's all that I did. I'm so sorry. Jan Sawyer

Mariani handed the note to Agent Moore. "Well, I guess that solves one mystery. But it looks like she didn't have anything to do with redirecting that drone or else she would have admitted it here."

"You're right Jenny. That helps Sander's group, but doesn't absolve them completely. Let's hope those new encryption schemes prevent any more hacking on the drones."

"I'll call Sanders and let him know about Sawyer. Send me a copy of Dr. Lee's autopsy."

"Right. Will do. Before we leave, we'll go through this condo and her computer to see if anything else turns up. I'll let you know."

"All right Tony. I'll see you back at the station."

Mariani and Pam Johnson go through the condo. Pam takes Sawyer's computer with her to analyze it. It looks like a suicide, just like Mariani had guessed. As they were driving back to the station, Pam asked Mariani why Sawyer did it.

"You know. Looks like youthful indiscretion. Someone offered her money to post some messages and for some reason, she thought that would be OK. Not to be indelicate Pam, but some of your generation seems to be a little too casual with information sharing."

"I know Tony. I can't believe what some of my friends post on Facebook. It's like they want the world to know everything going on in their life. Even boring stuff."

"I'm glad you're not like them Pam.

Chapter 31

For the first time, Noria Park met with her three field agents, Maria Ruiz, Sonya Niguel and Susan Kate in a Mexican restaurant in the city.

"You've all done perfectly in your assignments. Now we have the final task, to combine your efforts for one major attack."

Park opened up a large map of the city with annotations.

"We will simultaneously attack several areas of San Francisco at once. Sonya, you will launch a drone at the Bay Bridge, the busiest commuting bridge in the U.S. You'll launch the drone here, on the San Francisco side, at 6:00pm."

"When will I receive the drone?"

"We're going to hold that until the last moment, in order that you are not discovered. I'll give you that detail the day before."

"So we don't know what day this will happen?"

"No. None of you do. I'm keeping that secret to protect you all."

Park pointed to another part of the map.

"Maria, you will send fifty butterfly drones into Union Square. They will spray poison gas on shoppers."

"Finally, Susan, you will send a large drone with a chemical agent, into San Francisco's water supply. This combination of targets will confuse the authorities; they won't know who is behind this and the water supply will kill thousands before it's discovered."

"And what about the BART trains?"

"Oh, yes. We will stop all the BART trains the day before the attack. Thousands will have to commute the next day. That will maximize the effect of the Bay Bridge bombing."

"When do we meet again?"

"We don't. We will communicate the rest of the attack to you through these laptops. They are like burner phones. Untraceable. You may send and receive text messages here. Just make sure you are in a secure location when you use them, not out in public."

Park didn't tell her agents the ultimate target. A drone was set up in Marin to destroy the Golden Gate Bridge, in a coordinated attack with the bombing of the Bay Bridge. Thousands would be killed instantly.

Chapter 32

Sam Cho spent a lot of time in coffee shops with his laptop. As the senior technical adviser to the 7HTG, Sam valued his free time, away from all the top-secret security. He used his free time like most young people do, for social networking and dating. But even though his laptop looked like a regular computer, it was a highly secure product of the NSA, capable of intercepting secret communications.

"Hi, are you Sam?" Sam's blind date arrived at the coffee shop. He greeted her warmly.

"Hi Nancy. So glad to finally meet you. Please sit down."

First dates are usually awkward; especially blind dates, but Sam and Nancy were getting along wonderfully. About fifteen minutes into their conversation, Sam's laptop pinged a message.

Possible security risk with local computer.

Distracted now from Nancy, he opened up the message and tracked some disturbing comments from someone in the coffee shop. It was Susan Kate, openly discussing the terrorist attack with Noria Park. Sam recorded the conversation and marked it for surveillance.

"Did you hear what I said Sam? Aren't we going on another date?"

"I'm sorry Nancy. I have to go."

"Well, I'm sorry too. I thought you were different, not one of those computer nerds." Nancy leaves while Sam continues tracking the signal. Apparently, even though the laptops were secure in private, Sam's super computer was able to pull their signal through the WIFI, although no one else was able to see it.

Sam called Detective Mariani and asked him to come to the coffee shop. Mariani and Johnson were spending the Saturday in town. When they arrived, Mariani told Johnson to wait outside.

"Stay here Pam."

"All right Tony. Message me if you need anything."

Susan Kate was still there when he arrived. Sitting in a private corner, Sam explained to the Detective what he found.

"So it's someone in here planning an attack? Can you tell which computer and person?"

"Yes, it's that blonde woman over there. I've recorded all the details, even tracking the computer she is communicating with."

Mariani texted Pam Johnson

Pam, there is a tall blonde woman wearing navy blue yoga pants, a plaid skirt and a light blue top. Follow her when she leaves.

Pam confirms the task.

Sam Cho was a little nervous. "Can you contact Agent Moore?"

"Yes Sam, I'm doing that now. We'll just wait here until the blonde leaves. My partner will follow her and the FBI can pick her up from where she goes next. Sam, can you continue to track this computer?"

"Yes, anywhere in the world."

"Good, and the communications as well?"

"Now that I have the computer's technical information, it's all mine. I can even get into the hard disc."

"Good. Start looking. What about the computer she's communicating with?"

"Yup. I'll have any computer she contacts in my virtual hands. I can track all communications, even their locations."

Chapter 33

Detective Mariani, Sam Cho and Officer Johnson meet with Agent Moore in the San Francisco FBI field office. Agent Moore leads the meeting.

"Thanks to some luck, Sam Cho intercepted communications about an attack in San Francisco. With FBI agents support, we were able to identify the following people. Noria Park, Maria Ruiz, Sonya Niguel and Susan Kate. Noria Park was living with Robert Sanders; we suspect she planted a nano bug on Sanders' jacket. After the bug was discovered, Park disappeared, leaving Sanders' condo and her work in San Francisco."

"What about the others?"

"The three other women were part of a terrorist cell, planning a multi-target attack in two weeks."

"You haven't arrested them yet?"

"No. We have 24-hour surveillance on them, their homes and their movements while we continue to track communications among them through their computers. We have also tapped their cell phones."

"Did that tell you anything?"

"Yes, we found some old messages between Noria Park and Lisa Appleton, the prostitute who compromised Ted Eisenberg and Jan Sawyer."

"So Noria Park is the leader of this plot?"

"Yes and there's more. The CIA has found a tag between her and North Korea. We have to believe that they are behind this whole matter. We're attempting to intercept communications between Park and North Korea's secret intelligence group."

Chapter 34

Two days before the attack, the FBI arrested all the women and took them to separate locations for interrogation. Park, Ruiz and Niguel all kept silent, but Susan Kate caved under pressure. She provided confirmation of the attack and all the details about the others.

The FBI intercepted the weapons and arrested the delivery people. All in all, the capture included 23 people, mostly Koreans working in a secret terrorist cell in the Bay Area.

"Well, that's certainly not what I expected," said detective Laura Miller. Three hours earlier, David Bancroft, an English professor at Berkeley, had invited eight guests to his Victorian estate in Sonoma for a murder mystery dinner party.

"If only we had paid more attention to the clues," agreed Robert Warren, an attorney. "The solution was right in front of our face."

Laura shook her head, "the guys in the precinct are going to give me hell for missing this one."

David had carefully selected the diverse guest list to create a most spontaneous evening, like a fine chef who mixes seemingly incompatible ingredients and comes up with a masterly meal.

In addition to Laura and Robert, there was Elizabeth Ashley, a 28-year-old debutante turned socialite from Alabama. Her naturally golden hair, quiet elegance and refined grace were as intoxicating as her accent. Jim Palmer was a rookie police officer from Los Angeles, but his clean cut looks and baby face belied his intelligence and maturity. Dr. Jenny Song, a neurologist from Boston, looked more like a model than a brain surgeon. She was tall and athletic, with long straight black hair and a graceful gait. Which brings us to Father John Lopez, a Franciscan monk from San Diego and descendent of the original Spanish missionaries who settled California. John was not only a priest; he had a degree in philosophy from Harvard. Switching from the cerebral to the creative, Nancy Lee was a caterer from Marin, with a who's who list of wealthy clients from the golden county north of the Golden Gate Bridge; she was also very attractive with short hair, bangs, a button nose and sparkling eyes. To round out this gathering was Antonio Marini, a magician from Las Vegas. Antonio packed them in at the Desert Palm, with his incomprehensible illusion of making audience members disappear from the stage and show up seconds later at the back of the theater.

You might have noticed the one trait these people had in common, their refined looks. In fact, the guest list was as resplendent, alluring and beautiful as the mansion itself. Even Steven, the butler, was a tall, distinguished man with thick beard and mustache and Maria, the maid, a striking Latina in a French maid's outfit; perhaps these two were quiet, but significant characters in David's plans or merely servants. David never mentioned them in his bio of guests.

The last character was David's Victorian house, magnificently settled in his vineyard, an odd architecture for California. Unlike the homes in New England, this home was just a few years old, with hidden electronics behind a décor of old fashioned wallpaper, carpet, furnishings, artwork and adornments. David even infused an artificial, slightly musty smell into the rooms, another realistic but diverting element for the night. It would take a qualified appraiser more than a little while to uncover the veneer; exactly the way David had designed it.

The guests were all gathered in the library now, relaxing in leather chairs and soft sofas, looking each other over. Steven and Maria were serving drinks.

"So David" said Elizabeth, "when are you going to tell us about tonight's game?" David had sent out invitations that mentioned a mystery dinner party, but had not revealed much about the complexities to come.

"Certainly," said David. "We are here to solve a make believe murder that will occur sometime tonight. Each of you has received background information on the others, although none of you have ever met before. I have spent considerable time and money to insure that everyone here is an honorable person, not likely to cheat or otherwise ruin the game. Each of you will get one true and private clue to the identity of either the victim or the murderer, along with the clues that all of you may see or hear."

Elizabeth smiled and stroked her hair, Robert adjusted his glasses, Laura rubbed her palms together and Jim took out a pad to take notes. John sipped his wine and nodded in appreciation, loving the entertainment so lacking at the monastery.

"To win, you will have to uncover the identity of the murderer, the victim and how the murder was accomplished. The one who does that will also win $10,000 in cash. Oh yes, and I'm the only one who knows who the murderer and victim are."

Antonio rubbed the felt of his top hat, so common a home for doves in a magician's act. Nancy straightened her chef coat, not sure why she was asked to wear it. Jenny held her stethoscope in her white lab coat, and then asked the question they were all thinking. "David, why are we all dressed this way?"

"Ah, yes doctor. You are all dressed in your work attire. Nancy is a chef, John is a priest, Robert is a lawyer, Laura a detective, Elizabeth is a socialite, Jim is a police officer and Antonio is a magician, all of you at the top of your profession, destined for great lives and accomplishments. But tonight will challenge all of your creative and intellectual skills."

David adjusted his tweed deerstalker, the hat Sherlock Holmes made famous. "As I am the host of the game and a professor, I've selected this hat and pipe from my favorite detective. Now listen carefully to a few rules. You may go anywhere in the house, attic or basement and you must leave the company of the group at least once during the evening. But you may not leave the house. That would automatically disqualify you."

Robert pointed to the large rectangular frame, maybe 80" in diameter, above the library entrance. "And what is this, an empty picture frame?"

David held up a remote control. "That, my dear barrister, is a video monitor, another source of clues for everyone. There is a smaller monitor in each of the rooms, usually above the entering door." David pushed a button and the monitor revealed a view of the outside grounds, then the upstairs rooms, then the first floor rooms and finally the wine cellar. "The house may look old, but the electronics are state of the art. At various random times, the monitors will show you what is going on in different parts of the house, where others may be exploring for clues. Each room is also equipped with speakers, adding to the ambiance and providing audio clues. You see I have an obsession with murder mysteries, especially the sights and sounds of dark and stormy nights."

David pushes another button and a loud clap of thunder comes through the speakers while lightning reflected on the guests.

Robert was the first to comment on the weather anomaly. "I see, because we don't get storms up here."

David nodded. "Yes Robert, I may have saved some money if I bought my house in Seattle."

Jenny held up a Bluetooth earpiece. "And this, David?"

David pointed to the device. "Yes Jenny, each of you has one. During the night, you each will get a clue to the identity of the victim or the murderer."

Laura spoke up. "Are the clues private for us?"

David liked the way his guests were engaged. "No one else will hear your personal clue, but if you choose to share it, you are more likely to become the victim than the one who solves the crime."

The doorbell rings and a deliveryman hands Steven a shoebox-sized package wrapped in plain brown paper. "I'll just put this upstairs sir," said Steven.

David nodded. "Very good Steven. That package won't be needed tonight."

Jim offered his first question. "Are there any other restrictions David?"

David took out his notes and replied. "You may ask anyone anything, work together or by yourself. If a door is locked you must find a key or another way in, but remember, you can't leave the house." Another flash of lightning, the sound of thunder and a woman's scream is heard.

John jokes. "That wasn't Steven, was it?" There is laughter all around, and then the lights go out for 30 seconds. When they come back on, Antonio and Laura are missing.

Jenny was most concerned. "Maybe we have already learned who the murderer and victim are."

Nancy, realizing that this was just a diversion, bubbled. "Sounds like a delicious evening. I can't wait to start." Steven comes down the stairs; he joins Maria in the kitchen to begin serving. A grandfather clock rings six times.

"That's our cue for dinner" said David. As the guests meander from the library to the dining room, the monitor shows Antonio and Laura upstairs talking, but only Jenny notices this.

The guests find their place card and sit down. Laura returns to the dining room.

"Where were you?" said Jim.

Laura replied. "I heard footsteps; I thought it might be the killer."

Robert excuses himself. "Before we eat, I need to be excused."

Elizabeth puts her drink down. "I think I will step out for a minute too."

As they leave, Antonio comes back in and John questions him. "So you're back. What did you hear Antonio?"

Antonio points to his arm. "Nothing, somebody pulled on my arm when the lights went out and I ran after them."

A spotlight highlights a drapery sash and a chime is heard. The sash looks like a rope, but not everyone notices this clue. Jim makes a quick note on his pad, out of view.

Then Jim leaves the table. "I need to see where that scream came from."

Jenny joins him. "I'll go with you." They head upstairs.

David states the obvious. "Well, it looks like everyone is getting their time away from the group done early. Maria, you may start serving the soup."

Laura compliments David. "I think you have created one hell of a mystery David." The dining room monitor shows a male and female figure kissing, but in silhouette.

"More than you can imagine Laura. May I remind you, don't trust anyone." Spooky owl sounds emanate from the speakers, then the lights go out again and another scream is heard. A full minute passes in darkness. When the lights come on, Robert, Elizabeth, Jenny and Jim have returned.

Elizabeth speaks out as if she had never left. "What was that?"

David points them back to their seats. "Oh nothing, let's sit down everyone. The first course is ready, French onion soup." As Maria serves the soup, Steven pours dinner wine, a selection from David's own vineyard.

"Absolutely gourmet David" said Antonio; "did Steven or Maria make this?"

With a wink to Nancy, David explained. "Actually this feast is courtesy of our resident chef, Nancy. Don't worry; she made sure that no one's allergies would be affected."

A spotlight shines briefly on the candlestick of the centerpiece accompanied by a soft chime. Everyone at the table sees this clue and eyes the others.

With worried looks around the table, Nancy says, "It was prepared at my restaurant and brought here."

Antonio says what most of them are thinking. "You mean we have been eating food prepared by someone who could be the murderer?"

Elizabeth agreed. "That is outrageous! Why didn't you say something?"

Robert punctuated the point. "Bad form David. We may have missed a valuable clue."

David countered. "Actually, you have all missed several clues already. You didn't think this was going to be easy, did you?"

Just as John was about to speak, he heard a chime in his earpiece and his personal clue to the murder.

*AS A MAN OF FAITH, YOU KNOW THAT WHAT IS VISIBLE
MAY NOT BE TRUE. PEOPLE WILL TRY TO FOOL YOU
WITH LIES AND DECEPTION. HAVE FAITH! YOUR CLUE
IS THAT THE VICTIM PLAYS A PROMINENT PART IN THE
GAME.*

With this information, John realizes that Steven and
Maria are probably not directly involved. He compliments
Nancy. "This is excellent Nancy. Where is your restaurant?"

Nancy was happy to oblige the privileged guests. "In
San Francisco, near Ghirardelli Square. I made the dessert
especially for you Padre."

Laura jokes. "A Peach Bomb Surprise?"

Nancy continued. "Not quite. Alternate layers of angel
and devil's food cake. I call it *The Devil's Orchestra.*"

John smiles. "I can't wait. I'll finally be able to
separate good from evil." Everyone laughs.

Jim kids him, "You mean play God, John?"

John was enjoying this. "I thought that was something
you did son. Serve the good and punish the wicked."

Robert added his twist. "Well, Jim stops them, Laura
investigates them and I put them away. You could call us a
crime team."

Antonio adds his opinion; "your team seems to have an
advantage in this game, being expert investigators."

Robert turns the accusation back to Antonio. "And you
are an expert at misdirection and disguise. Do you have a
weapon up your sleeve?"

Antonio couldn't resist. "No, just a rabbit;" and he pulls a rabbit out for everyone's enjoyment.

Jim has a fake look of concern. "What kind of soup did you say this was?" Antonio frees the rabbit and it runs out of the room.

"Will he be all right?" said Elizabeth.

Antonio reassured her. "Oh yes, he'll find some warm spot and go to sleep. Rabbits are very good pets, you know."

"What do you say David?" said Robert. "Does anyone here have an advantage in solving the mystery?"

David is glad this question came up. "Not in the least. In fact, our expert investigators will probably think too much, making their conclusions faulty."

At this point Antonio gets up, takes Maria aside and asks "excuse me dear, where is the rest room?"

Maria responds politely. "The door next to the kitchen is closest sir."

Antonio puts his arm around her waist, whispers something, winks and then walks to the bathroom. Out of sight from the others, he sees a lead pipe in the kitchen spotlighted with that soft chime sound. "This may be an extra clue just for me," he says to himself.

Everyone is impressed by the soup and congratulates Nancy. "This tastes Mediterranean. Is that the region of your cuisine?" said Elizabeth.

"Well, it's a fusion restaurant combining Mediterranean with Asian flavors. Even though I was trained in China, I also spent two years in Italy and that's when I decided to blend these heavenly foods into one cuisine."

David agreed. "Eating at your restaurant has elevated my palate Nancy. This is one reason I invited you to the game, to show these guests that we have world class chefs in the bay area."

Jenny hears a chime in her earpiece but places her hand over it secretly in order to hide the fact that her personal clue was coming.

DO NOT JUMP TO CONCLUSIONS. DON'T TRUST YOUR EYES OR EARS. TO WIN THIS GAME YOU WILL NEED TO FIND FACTS. REMEMBER, PEOPLE LIE AND FORGET. YOUR CLUE IS THAT THE MURDER WEAPON WILL BE FOUND.

Her clue finishes just before loud thunderclaps resonate through the house. The lights go out again for another minute. A gunshot is heard along with the sound of a body hitting the floor. When the lights come back on, Steven is lying motionless on the floor. The rabbit has snuggled under his leg and there are hairs on Steven's trousers. Then we see Antonio return from the kitchen.

Elizabeth screams, points and says, "Look, it's the butler."

Jenny rushes over to check his vital signs. As everyone comes closer, Jenny holds a card up that says VICTIM, truly a sign of relief. "Well, I guess this means the butler is dead. You are dead Steven, aren't you?"

Steven looks up and replies "yes doctor. Thank you for confirming it." The butler looks at David. "Since my part of the game is done sir, would you mind if I went to my room to take a nap? I don't think I can lie still for five hours."

Everyone looks at David and in unison says "Five hours?"

David ignores their complaint. "Of course not. Quite right Steven. Buttle off to your room." He leaves with the VICTIM card and the rabbit under his arm to his upstairs room.

Expecting this interruption, David announces. "Let's return to dinner. Maria, I'm afraid you're going to have to serve by yourself."

Nancy volunteers. "Nonsense, I am glad to help you. I believe the crabmeat stuffed in lobster mushrooms are next."

Maria curtseys to Nancy. "Thank you for your help Ma'am" and they go into the kitchen.

Jenny says, "I believe lobster mushrooms are poisonous."

David tries to reassure everyone. "Really Jenny? I can guarantee you that no one will really die tonight."

Elizabeth adds, "Well, at least we know that the butler didn't do it." Laughter breaks the tension.

While Nancy and Maria serve the appetizers, Robert wants to hear more about the mushrooms. "Nancy, someone is concerned about the lobster mushrooms."

Nancy clarifies. "No, these are porcini mushrooms, cut in the shape of a lobster. They're perfectly safe," then winks at everyone cheekily.

A spotlight shines briefly on a hypodermic needle on the sideboard, then that soft chime sounds. Only a few of the guests notice it.

Jim saw the hypodermic needle and was watching the others. "Since we are part of a murder mystery, I'd like to ask John about the nature of good and evil."

John gestured with his hand. "Well, I certainly believe in good and evil. You see all sorts of unimaginable crimes against people because of anger, greed, envy and lust."

Jenny inquires "the deadly sins padre?" then John continues.

"That's right Jenny, along with gluttony, sloth and pride, but those three don't usually lead to violence."

As Maria and Nancy serve the appetizers, Laura shares her experience. "I think drugs are the problem. Nearly every violent criminal I have investigated was involved with illegal substances, either using or selling them."

John adds "yes, but before that. What sends a person down that path to drugs and violence?"

Jim had his opinion. "Lack of education, poor parenting, drug use at home. It all begins in the home. If parents take care of their children and raise them right, drugs or gangs won't tempt them. And it's not limited to the poor. I know many poor families doing a great job at raising children."

John kept the topic philosophical. "But what about faith? What about a person's conscience? Why do some people resist the temptation of crime while others succumb to it?"

David notices that wineglasses are empty. "Maria would you please go to the wine cellar and get us another couple bottles?"

Maria nods and says "right away sir." Jenny offers to go with her. They exit though the basement door.

126

Elizabeth brought them back to the conversation. "Are you saying that some people are born good and some are born bad?"

John answered, "What I am saying is that we have free will. We all have choices to make. Those who make bad choices follow a path that leads to crime, or in extreme cases, even eternal damnation."

Laura agreed. "So everyone is responsible for his or her own actions."

John nodded. "Remember, people don't choose evil for evil's sake. They are mistaken into thinking they are choosing happiness. This is how Satan deceives man."

Robert wonders what happened to Maria and Jenny. "I think I'll see what we have for a wine selection."

"Aren't some people pushed beyond their limit, their ability to make good choices? What about someone who steals to feed his family" said Elizabeth?

John added. "Yes, that seems like a paradox, stealing to feed your family. The fault lies in trying to understand the will of God. We are limited in our capacity to do so. Certainly the injustices of the world are one of those mysteries."

A spotlight flashes briefly on a dagger hidden into the wallpaper, only the men hearing the chime in time to see the dagger. "What was that?" said Elizabeth, "what clue was shown?" No one was willing to answer.

Laura asked, "So why do good people fall out of God's grace?"

John responded. "Man is an imperfect being, subject to sin throughout his life here. This is not the kingdom of Heaven. This world is where Satan's lies and deceptions lead men astray. Only a focus on Christ and the word of God can repel the power of Satan."

"But how many people can do that?" Laura asked John.

"Actually, no one can. That's where grace comes in. Sometimes we are being protected without realizing it. But if you know something is wrong, then you have an obligation to resist it."

Jim agreed. "I'm with the Padre. If you resist evil, you'll get help from above. Maybe angels, maybe something else. But if you look for trouble, you will certainly find it."

John was slowly winning over the others. "Very true Jim. How many of us can say they haven't looked for trouble now and then?"

Laura asked John. "Even you Padre? Have you looked for trouble?"

John paused, remembering a time in his life when he was troubled. "Before I entered the seminary, I was almost lost to the dark side. My friends robbed a bank. Unfortunately, I was in the getaway car. The police caught them before they got to the car. When I heard gunshots, I took off out of there."

Jim didn't think John could have been involved. "So you didn't know they were going to rob a bank?"

John was relieved to clear this up. "No and my friends never gave me up. They either wanted to protect me or knew it wouldn't help them, maybe both."

"You're lucky Padre. Today, with DNA, we would have brought you in," said Jim.

At this point, Maria, Jenny and Robert return, each straightening their clothing. Jenny and Robert take their seats while Maria pours new wine.

"So that's when you decided to join the priesthood?" said Laura.

"No, things got even worse for me. A drunk driver killed my sister. She had just gotten engaged and was coming home from her shower."

Jenny was visibly upset. "That's terrible John. I'm so sorry."

"Between escaping the bank robbery and the injustice of my sister's death, my world was turned upside down. That's when I started looking for answers."

Laura asked "but you must have known that these circumstances had nothing to do with you."

"I know," said John. "But in my mind, you can either believe in free will or fate?"

"Can't you believe in both" said Laura.

John thought for a moment. "Maybe. I personally think that man has free will, except for the important things in life." The discussion was interrupted when Elizabeth hears her clue coming.

SOCIAL PARTIES ARE YOUR HOME FIELD. YOU KNOW HOW TO READ PEOPLE. DON'T BE FOOLED BY FIRST IMPRESSIONS. YOUR CLUE IS THAT THE MURDERER'S NAME HAS FIVE LETTERS.

"My friends and that drunk driver had free will. They decided to do what they did. But their decisions affected me greatly and after my sister's death, I started to drink. It was only a year later when I realized I was self-destructing."

Jim asked. "You mean you were falling victim to Satan?"

"Yes. That's when I joined the seminary. I knew I needed a lot more than my own will power to survive. The order showed me how to protect myself and to help others."

Although Robert understood the subtleties of John's philosophy, he worked in a world where judgments were made in a black or white manner that is guilty or not guilty. "I can't afford to make such distinctions. It doesn't matter whether or not someone had free will, only that they understood the difference between right and wrong."

Nancy and Maria bring out the main course: Asian duck marinated in a marsala sauce, risotto and finely cut vegetables inside of mu shu pancakes with hoisin sauce. Nancy announces "Bon appetite everyone!" The main course was a most welcome way to lighten the ambiance with more carnal pleasures. There was applause and pleasant comments as the food was set in front of everyone. The seriousness of John's good and evil sermon was replaced with small talk and gentility.

As they were finishing their dinner, the grandfather clock struck seven times. The sounds of owls, thunder and rain are audible throughout the house now. Most of the guests had not heard their personal clue and their senses were heightened as they prepared to solve the mystery. Was John's loquaciousness an attempt to divert attention from his true role as the murderer? What about the long absence of Maria, Jenny and Robert in the basement? How long could it take to find a couple bottles of wine? Antonio slipped out of sight for a while; and who brings a rabbit to a dinner party? Is it possible that the murderer has an accomplice? The only undisputable clue was that Steven was the victim. Finding the murderer will indeed be more difficult, as David had warned. Speaking of David, could he be the murderer?

With dinner finished and dessert to come later, the guests return to the library. The video monitor is now a focal point for clues. Maria is doing double duty, serving after dinner drinks and cleaning up the dining room table.

Elizabeth was the first to reiterate appreciation for the meal. "That dinner was divine Nancy. You can expect me at your restaurant before heading home."

Nancy was humbled. "Just let me know; I'll get you a table with a view of the bridge."

Robert made a suggestion. "I say we all gather there for a celebration with the winner picking up the tab."

Nancy liked the idea. "I'll even give you the murderer's discount."

None of the guests needed (or in John's case wanted) the $10,000, so the atmosphere was generally convivial and more a friendly test of intellect, a game rich people play for amusement between their careers and obligations. As everyone settled down with their cognac and other aperitifs, Robert heard a chime in his earpiece and his clue.

AS A LAWYER, YOU SEE LIARS EVERYDAY. SOMEONE WILL TRY TO DECEIVE YOU. TREAT THEM AS YOU WOULD AN ADVERSARY. DO YOUR OWN RESEARCH AND DON'T ASK ANY QUESTIONS YOU DON'T ALREADY KNOW THE ANSWERS TO. YOUR CLUE IS THAT THE MURDERER IS NOT AFRICAN-AMERICAN.

Robert looked up, muttered to himself "Really?" and surmised that he wasn't being given as much help as the others.

"Did you get your clue Robert?" said Laura.

"Yes, but it wasn't that enlightening. Does anyone want to share their clues?" There were general smiles and silence all around. "That's what I thought. Then I'll just keep mine to myself too."

Laura couldn't contain her detective instincts. "While we're waiting for dessert, I think we should start exploring the house, looking for evidence. Jim, would you like to join me?"

Jim readily agreed, comfortable working with a detective. "Sure Laura", pulling out his small notepad, "I need a lot more information." Laura and Jim went upstairs.

A spotlight shows a wrench in a toolkit in the corner of the room, and the sound of the soft chime. Only Nancy and Antonio seemed to see the wrench and subtly look in another direction. "Did anyone see what the chime announced?" said Antonio, diverting attention away from him while trying to finesse information from the others. Shaking heads and silence were the response.

"Nancy, would you like to explore with me?" he said. Having completed her kitchen duties, she agreed.

"Sure, sounds like an adventure." They take the other stairway upstairs, on the opposite side of the house behind the location of the video monitor.

Robert decides to stay and make notes on his tablet. "I think I'll just consider the facts from here for now." He discovers that the house has a high-speed Wi-Fi connection as well, not at all surprising, but something that may be useful in his research.

Elizabeth gives Jenny a flirting glance, and then asks. "Jenny, you're kind of a detective, examining patients and looking for clues for a diagnosis."

Jenny replies to Elizabeth but addresses everyone. "I suppose so. But I'm not sure of anything except that Steven is the victim." Then turning to David. "Do you think that there could be more than one murder?"

David stroked his chin. "It certainly is possible, but I won't say any more than that."

At this point, the silhouetted figures of two people kissing are visible in the monitor. "Look" said Robert, so that everyone would get this clue.

John then decides he would like to go upstairs. "I think I'll explore by myself. This is one time I don't trust anyone" laughing at his own comment. He starts by going into the kitchen, although there are stairs to the basement and second floor from there.

Robert looked at David. "Aren't you going to search the house?"

David replied "no need. I'm sure I'm not the murderer and I can't win the game."

Elizabeth walks by Jenny and whispers something into her ear. "Yes, I would like to find out what's going on upstairs too. Jenny, would you like to join me?"

Jenny makes eye contact and smiles. "Certainly, at least to keep an eye on the others." They take the stairway. Halfway up the stairs, Elizabeth takes Jenny by the hand, although only Robert noticed this fact.

David asked Robert, "You don't seem to be in a hurry to explore."

Robert looked up from his tablet. "I think the answer to this mystery lies in watching others, listening to what they say and do and what they don't say, like in court."

David smiles. "You may have the right strategy Robert. Good luck."

Laura comes back downstairs holding a bloody dagger with a gloved hand. "You might be interested to see what I found in the attic."

Robert asks nervously "David, I hope that isn't real blood."

David replies "of course not, just a piece of the puzzle." Before they could continue positing about the significance of the dagger, the lights go out. We hear thunder and footsteps. There is the shadow of a person running outside, past the first floor window.

Although still in darkness, Robert points it out to Laura. "Did you see that?"

Laura quickly deduced the significance. "Yes. That person was outside the house. If it were one of us, they would forfeit the game. We should be able to detect rain on their clothing."

The lights come back on and Nancy returns as well announcing another discovery. "I found a clue. This rope was under a bed upstairs."

Forgetting that she was involved in a game, Laura responded in her normal role as a detective. "Give that to me. There may be skin cells on it."

Robert contradicted her theory. "Come now Laura. You can't believe there has been an actual murder here, do you?"

Laura took a yard size white cloth out of her pocket, laid the dagger and rope on it and said "I'll just keep an open mind until we have some answers."

Nancy hears a chime in her earpiece and listens for her clue.

YOUR SEARCH HAS BEEN REWARDED. YOU FOUND A CLUE TO THE IDENTITY OF THE VICTIM. THE ROPE WAS PLACED UNDER THE BED BY THE MURDERER TO DISTRACT YOU. YOUR CLUE IS THAT THE VICTIM WAS POISONED.

Not wanting to let anyone know she got a clue, she quickly changed the attention back to Laura. "By the way, wasn't Jim with you?"

Laura responded naturally. "Yes, but we split up to cover more rooms. Wasn't Antonio with you?"

Nancy gave her answer quickly. "He pulled a disappearing act. I turned around and he had just vanished. Ironic for a magician, yes?"

Robert tried to put in a puzzle piece. "We saw the shadow of someone run across that window. It could have been Antonio."

Laura added "or Jim, John, Elizabeth or Jenny. We will know more when everyone returns."

Just as his name was mentioned, John returned from the kitchen, holding a small bottle of liquid labeled *Aconitum*. "I found this hidden in a kitchen cabinet. Nancy, is there any reason this would be used in cooking?"

Nancy had never heard of the substance. "Not that I know of. David, is this a clue?"

David took the bottle, read the label and then opened it. "Well, let's see" and he took a sip, shocking his guests. "Well, I guess it's not real poison."

Laura realized the same fact. "Let's put it on the table with the dagger and rope." Then she heard the chime in her earpiece and her personal clue.

JUST BECAUSE YOU ARE A DETECTIVE, DO NOT ASSUME THAT YOU ARE ABOVE SUSPICION. IN FACT, SOMEONE IS TRYING TO LEAD OTHERS IN YOUR DIRECTION. YOUR CLUE IS THAT THE MURDERER IS A MAN.

Robert summed it up. A dagger, rope and poison, but no gun. Wasn't Steven killed by a gunshot?"

Laura assumed so. "He must have been shot. I heard the gun. Let's look for it."

Robert held up his hand. "Wait a minute. Jim's in uniform and I think he's armed."

Jim returns to find the others staring at him. "Jim, we think your gun was used to kill Steven."

Jim is shocked. "No, it wasn't," showing his gun. Jim empties the bullets out and one is missing. "Someone is trying to frame me. This gun hasn't been fired."

Then Laura says, "Let me see your gun officer." Jim hands her the gun. "He's right. This gun hasn't been fired."

Jim was relieved to hear Laura defend him and now he hears a chime with his clue.

AS A POLICE OFFICER, YOU PROBABLY EXAMINED ALL OF THE EVIDENCE, BUT WHAT YOU DIDN'T KNOW WILL HELP YOU SOLVE THE CRIME. YOUR CLUE IS THAT THE VICTIM IS A MAN.

"But this one has" said Jenny as she comes into the room. "I found this one upstairs and it's still smoking."

Robert's expression is incredulous. "A smoking gun. Really?"

Jenny hands Laura the gun. "Well, this may be smoking, but it's not a real gun. It's a starter pistol, but it sounds like the real thing." Laura puts the gun on the table with the dagger, rope and poison.

Antonio and Elizabeth return. "What's going on?" said Antonio. Then he hears the chime in his earpiece.

YOU ARE PROBABLY WONDERING WHY IT TOOK SO LONG TO GET YOUR CLUE, BUT YOUR PATIENCE WILL PAY OFF. YOUR CLUE IS THAT THE MURDERER LEFT THE HOUSE DURING THE GAME.

Steven enters the library with a bag of money, the kind you saw in the old monopoly game with an oversized dollar sign on it. "Here you go sir."

David took the bag. "Thank you Steven. It's time for each of you to guess the name of the murderer."

Jim was first to guess. "Well, let's look at our clues. We have a dagger with blood on it, a rope, a bottle of poison and a gun." I think it is Antonio. He was missing at some key times and he's the only one I can't account for."

Jenny agreed. "Yes, I think it was Antonio too."

Laura was the only real detective here. Surely her guess would be correct. "I think it was Jim. Even though we ruled his gun out as the weapon, he could have used the starter pistol earlier." Antonio and Nancy readily got on board with Laura's guess.

Robert added his thoughts. "But what about the person we saw running across the window? And why didn't anyone have rain on his or her clothing? I think it was Elizabeth. She was out quite a bit."

John agreed with Robert. "Yes, Elizabeth. She was out a couple times."

Elizabeth was surprised to hear she was being accused. She knew she didn't murder Steven. "Well, I happen to know the murderer's name had five letters. It was my personal clue, so I think it had to be Nancy. After all, there was poison in the kitchen."

David gave everyone the answer they had been waiting for. "You're all wrong! Actually, Steven was the murderer. He poisoned ME with the soup. But since I am required to manage the game, I could not divulge my secret until now. Remember the directions I gave you in the beginning. Only personal clues are accurate; whatever else you see, hear or infer could be misleading. You are likely to see and hear many things. Don't trust anyone."

Elizabeth objected. "Wait, my clue was that the murderer's name had five letters."

Then David explained. "Yes, Steven has five letters. S T E V and N. The E is used twice."

David points to Steven. "He doesn't have rabbit hairs on his trousers anymore because he changed clothing when he came inside from the rain. His clothing was dry and there weren't any rabbit hairs from when the rabbit cuddled up against him earlier. This means that no one here was correct and this money will go to charity." The guests applauded David for his generosity and asked about having another game next year.

Nancy's refined sense of smell alerted her. "Something smells funny."

Robert looked up. "It's coming from upstairs."

Jim heads upstairs and returns with the package delivered earlier. "The smell is definitely coming from this package." While Jim took a note out from brown paper wrapping, the guests looked at each other, while grimacing with the increasingly putrid smell.

"What does it say Jim?" People are holding their noses now, making exaggerated sounds of disgust. Jim reads the note out loud.

"To our detectives. I know you have all done your best to solve our mystery. Here's some final food for thought." Jim opens the box to show everyone the rotting contents. *"I hope you enjoyed the red herrings."*

With no winner, the guests finish their drinks and have dessert. During the evening, acquaintances became friends and promises were made to keep in touch. A date to get together at Nancy's restaurant was confirmed. David joins the others in an oversized limousine and Steven drives everyone to a jazz club in San Francisco.

Mozart's chamber music emanated from the room speakers. The ominous sounds of owls, thunder and footsteps are gone. The sound of rain has been replaced by the swishing of washing dishes and the wind gusts by the vacuuming of carpets. Although no one was ever in danger, the house has taken on a peaceful, if not sedate, demeanor. Finally, Maria has finished putting away the dishes and is wiping down the excess water around the sink when she hears a chime. She pauses and looks at the speaker above her head when a voice comes on.

WOULD YOU LIKE TO JOIN ME FOR A DRINK?

The Waiting Room

Amy had been in many waiting rooms. Car service centers, banks, hospitals, etc. But the strangest waiting room she had ever been to was in her doctor's office in one of those professional suites. Amy walked up for her appointment and saw yards of heavy plastic secured around the entrance and outside windows, maybe 20 feet wide. There was a sign on the door.

Please excuse our appearance as we remodel.

We are expanding to serve you better.

An arrow pointed to the right of the door to a temporary entrance. Apparently, her doctor's practice was doing very well.

"I'm here for my 2:30pm appointment; my name is Amy Eng." The medical assistant looked on her computer screen. "Here you are. I see you're a little early. While we are remodeling, our temporary waiting room is over there." The receptionist pointed to a small room down the hallway.

Amy walked into the room and saw office furniture that was older than she was. Plaid, orange and gray fabric over veneer oak armchairs, a black leatherette couch, a cheesy plastic table and the requisite middle class magazines, none from the 21st century. On the wall were paint by number pictures of clowns in cheap frames, an Ansel Adams photograph that looked like it was taken out of a magazine and one of those certificates proving that the doctor had actually been trained. The rug was industrial grade, tightly woven, charcoal in color with specks of yellow. There were no windows and a stale smell.

A young woman in blue scrubs came in and removed one of the chairs. Amy sat on the couch and watched. The woman returned and took another chair. Amy looked around. Then the woman came back and started removing the pictures. There was no one else in the room to commiserate with. The woman took the plastic table, the magazines and the framed certificate. Soon the only thing remaining was Amy and the leatherette couch. She didn't mind the removal of the eyesore furnishings, the ancient magazines, the clown pictures or the certificate. Then a man, dressed in green scrubs, came in with the woman, holding a straight back, wooden chair. "We're going to have to take the couch. Would you mind sitting here for a moment?"

Amy acquiesced silently. She realized that this must be someone else's office that her doctor was taking over. She looked around the room, then at her watch. Surely the doctor would be seeing her soon. "Wait a minute," she said to herself, only slightly audibly. "Is this still a waiting room?" She looked down the hallway. "Hello, is anyone here?" No reply or for that matter any sound. Amy walked back to the receptionist's desk. The office was vacant, without life, like something out of a French existentialist story. Then a horrible thought occurred to Amy.

She was missing.

The Old Man and the Sea

Tony walked his old dog Sam through the fog in Gig Harbor, down by the boats and past the colorful kayaks standing like toy soldiers, waiting for tourists. Nothing had opened yet. The fog absorbed his mind and body. He could feel moisture on his face and hands. Pausing to take some hot chocolate from his thermos, he wished he had eaten before his walk. The fog didn't care. It comes and goes as it pleases. The sun had already risen, but there weren't any cracks in the fog to prove it. The sun waits for the fog to disappear, too slowly for children and too quickly for artists.

Sam wasn't in any hurry. He reached the age when walking was difficult, when younger dogs ran around him and encouraged him to play, but Sam would just lay down and watch them fetch balls or catch Frisbees with their young families. It wouldn't be long before Sam would be joining Tony's wife, resting in peace. Tony and Sam seemed to have that in common, time having caught up with them.

The harbor was changing. Older businesses like a shoe repair shop, a newsstand and a laundry mat had been replaced by upscale eateries, Starbucks and a hot yoga studio. At least there weren't any pot shops yet, not in Gig Harbor.

Tony walked past a new art gallery. Progressive paintings for the new upper middle class moving into town. No still life or fruit pictures here, but more modern looks at nature and the environment. Art had to have a message now.

Artists love the fog. It blankets the noise and commotion of life. It quiets the mind. It did the same for Tony. But Tony wasn't an artist. He loved to read, but never wrote. He loved paintings, but never painted. He loved music but never played an instrument. This had become one of his life regrets, having never experienced the joy of creativity. He wiped a tear from his eye. No one was there to see it.

Loneliness and regret are brothers who have lived long, but uneventful lives. Their quiet existence hides more powerful emotions, like anger and silent ones like melancholy. He guessed those were his choices now, to be angry or despondent. But that only made him feel more depressed. So while the fog provided inspiration for the authors, painters and musicians, it only served to accent his life of mediocrity.

Tony wasn't poor. He had saved a bit of money from a small printing business he had started. Now, when he had the time to enjoy it, he didn't know what to do. His wife of forty years had died a year ago. Their only child, a daughter, lived on the other coast, busy with a family of her own. She would visit once or twice a year, unless something came up. He could afford to visit her, but after a day or so, he felt like he was intruding.

Tony returned from the quiet, foggy harbor to his home, an old bungalow half a mile uphill. The drab grey exterior needed painting and the gutters were filled with leaves from the oak tree in the backyard. He was able to afford the house after leaving the service in 1971, thanks to the GI bill. Ten thousand dollars back then, but paid for now. Expensive housing was going up around the harbor, as tech professionals found Gig Harbor the place to go instead of overpriced Seattle.

With his wife and business gone, Tony was feeling depressed. Maybe it was also the fog and the endless rain that came down in this Washington port town? Should he just hop a flight to San Diego? Would that lift his spirits? He had nothing to lose.

***

Getting off the plane at John Wayne Airport, he rented a sports car, a red convertible, with black leather seats. With the top down and the sun shining warmly on his arms and face, he felt a little better. Finding a 60s radio station, he began to relax. Then he pulled into Hilo Hattie, a Hawaiian clothing store. He left with enough Socal clothing for a week and even bought a pair of Maui Jim sunglasses. Tony had transformed his look to match his new surroundings. He smiled as he got back into his car.

Next stop was the happiest place on Earth. He drove among the families parking in those character-based lots, watching children tug their parents toward the park. He was directed to a spot in '*Happy*', perhaps the mark of a good day. A woman saw him get out of the expensive sports car, walking to the tram pick up stop. She made sure she could sit next to him.

"Hi. My name is Shannon."

Tony was startled by this forward woman, who wasn't unattractive. She must have been in her early 40s, with long reddish brown hair, tied back with a red scrunchy. Her jeans looked new and she wore a light blue Danskin underneath a loose fitting peasant shirt. She was clearly a former flower child, a product of the 60s. Tony extended his hand.

"I'm Tony. Nice to meet you."

"What a great day for the park, don't you think?"

"Yes, I haven't seen sunshine for a month."

"Oh, why is that?"

"I'm from Washington State and it's the rainy season. Where are you from?"

"San Diego."

Shannon was fudging a bit. She was actually from Dulzura (population 700), a town made famous by Clark's Pickelized Figs, a company that went out of business due to a sugar shortage during World War I.

"Sounds lovely. I've always wanted to visit there. What do you do?"

Shannon continued to fudge. "I'm in the honey business."

Actually, she had just sold her hives to the company that was really in the honey business. Then she bought some new clothes, packed a bag and headed to Anaheim looking for excitement.

"That's very interesting. Do I know your brand?"

"Have you heard of Temecula Valley honey?"

Shannon held her breath after this lie.

"No, sorry. I guess they don't ship to the Northwest."

Shannon smiled and sighed. "No, mostly Southern California. Actually, I just sold my business. That's why I'm here, to relax."

Tony was warming up to this former hippie. Imagine meeting a California flower girl from the 60s.

"What do you do Tony?"

Tony also managed to massage the truth. "I just sold my graphic arts company, so I'm here to relax too."

Actually it was a small print shop, but was located on 100 feet of Gig Harbor waterfront, so a hotel company offered him $500,000 for the location, and then tore down his dilapidated shop.

Shannon was clearly impressed.

"Oh, graphic arts. Did you work with advertising agencies?"

Tony shifted his eyes slightly. "Of course."

Most of Tony's business actually consisted of those flyers kids put on your windshield for pizza and advertising the local dollar store.

"But we were getting a lot of competition from Seattle, so I decided to sell out and take it easy."

Shannon wondered how old Tony was. He had a full head of hair, not gray.

Maybe he's in his 50s.

"You're kind of young to retire, aren't you?"

Tony enjoyed the compliment. "Well, 57, not that young."

Tony was 64.

The tram pulled into the main gate and they got off together.

"Would you like some company?" Shannon said.

"A young girl like you want to spend time with an old man. You must be in your mid thirties."

Shannon was 43. "How did you guess? I'm 36. I would love company. Disneyland is always more fun when you're with someone."

They bought their tickets and walked down Main Street. Shannon nudged Tony toward the runaway train ride.

"Still like the roller coasters Tony?

"Of course."

During the twists and turns, Shannon snuggled close to him and held his hand, with the excitement of a teenager. Tony could smell her perfume and was able to glance at her breasts during the ride. Good thing he bought the loose fitting khakis. When the ride was over, he watched Shannon exit the train. She was about 5'8" with a few extra pounds, like him. When he exited, he could see a smile on her face.

"Splash Mountain?" she said animatedly, reaching out for Tony's hand.

"Sure. Let's go."

Tony and Shannon spent the morning getting to know each other, stopping for lunch at the French restaurant at California Adventure. As they sat outdoors under the umbrella, Tony started fantasizing about Shannon.

"Where are you staying?"

"Oh, I just came up from San Diego. I hadn't made arrangements yet."

Shannon had sold her beat up car, took the bus to Anaheim, with only a suitcase of essentials she had just purchased. Bathing suit, lingerie and casual clothing. Apparently, she was looking to start over, perhaps with this new man.

"Neither have I."

Tony dropped this as a way of finding out if they might be together that night, but Shannon hadn't given him enough information. Now it was his turn.

"I was thinking about the Grand Californian, trying to impress her."

Shannon let her leg slip against his under the table.

"That's a wonderful place. I've been there many times."

She hadn't.

"Yes, I've always stayed there when I'm here."

He hadn't.

They looked at each other, maintaining eye contact until one of them would speak next. Each decided it was too risky to make the next move, so they finished their lunch with quiet flirting.

"Cars land? Have you been on it?"

"Not yet. Sure, let's go."

Shannon managed to get Tony on all the fast rides where a couple could be next to each other. The twists and turns gave her a chance to slip closer, by accident, of course. Tony was invigorated by this woman, and gladly played along. Still wondering about the sleeping arrangements, he waited for the right time to ask.

Then, late afternoon, after they had rocked and rolled through all the turbulent rides, including the Tower of Terror, they entered the Haunted Mansion, just to rest a bit. The slow ride through the dark emboldened Tony to risk the question, but before he could ask, Shannon slid her hand over him in the most suggestive way.

Smiling, she asked. "Grand Californian?" while slowly rubbing the inside of his thigh.

Remaining as calm as possible, Tony reached over and kissed her. "The Grand Californian."

Reassured now, Shannon snuggled into Tony, put his arm around her and enjoyed the ride. "We should probably reserve our room."

So they walked up to the Main Street guest services building and made a reservation.

"How many nights sir?" said the young man wearing a plaid red vest, crisp white shirt and black bow tie.

Tony and Shannon looked at each other. He waited for her to speak. She whispered in Tony's ear.

"Four nights." Tony said with mixed feelings. This was going to cost quite a bit, but, well, I'm on vacation.

Shannon gave Tony a gentle pat on his bottom, unseen by the young man making the reservation behind his counter. He glanced at her and returned the gesture.

"And would you like to make a dinner reservation?"

Shannon spoke up this time. "Yes, about 8pm please."

Tony knew what that meant. Love making before and after dinner. Well, that would give him time to recover. But how much would she desire after that. He started to think of ways he could extend himself, to live up to his hopes and her expectations this night.

"Would you arrange for a bowl of fruit and some champagne on ice? We'll be arriving around 5:30."

"Very good sir. The room will be ready. Here is your confirmation."

Shannon squeezed Tony's hand, and he realized they were on the same page. No more guessing.

Tony and Shannon had built a wonderful fantasy, based on multiple lies, and neither of them was in any hurry to return to reality. So they continued to redefine themselves in the ultimate getaway from the real world.

There were only a couple more logistics. "Where is your car?"

"I took a limo here from San Diego. My bag is in a locker at the main gate."

"All right. Mine is in my car. Let's go get yours first."

Shannon realized her luggage wasn't fitting in with her new identity. "Why don't I meet you at the hotel? I'd like to get a few things first."

Tony agreed. "Sure. Meet you there to check in?"

Shannon gave Tony a short, but convincing kiss. "See you then."

Tony and Shannon split up for an hour. She went to upgrade her luggage and lingerie. Tony went to pick up some flowers and chocolate. After all, he was from a different generation.

Their room overlooked the Magic Kingdom. In addition to the fruit and champagne, Tony placed flowers and chocolate on the table. Shannon didn't take long to get comfortable.

"You must be tired after the day we had. Why don't we change into something more comfortable?" Shannon took her bag into one of the two bathrooms. Tony took a quick shower and came out in a hotel robe. He poured two glasses and opened the box of chocolate.

Shannon came out in a hotel robe too, but underneath she had a sexy red outfit. When she got closer, she opened the robe. "You like?"

Tony's heartbeat jumped a few decibels.

"I like very much." He handed her the glass and they drank. He fed her fruit and chocolate. Shannon noticed that Tony was beginning to get excited. She took his glass, put it down and led Tony to the bed. She held her robe open, requesting him to take it off. He did and took his off as well, leaving him just in his new underwear.

Shannon pulled down the covers, and lay down. "Come on lover. I'm ready."

Tony didn't have to be asked twice. Her body was even more alluring in the early evening as the sun had set with soft lighting from candles speckling the dark room. He tried not to be too aggressive but Shannon wanted to get going.

"Don't be shy. I've been thinking about this all day."

So, their first time in bed was intense. Tony liked that. He could smell her perfume, something he hadn't in years. She wore expensive make up too. Perhaps this woman is the start of something long term.

An hour later, they began getting dressed for dinner. Shannon walked into the bathroom and whispered in his ear.

"Now I know why they call this the happiest place on earth."

Tony kissed her lips. "Mmm. What is that flavor?"

"Something tropical. I'll tell you after dinner."

Tony and Shannon continued their fantasy for the next few days, exploring the parks, driving his sports car to the beach and even taking a day to visit museums in L.A. Both wondered where the end of their trip would lead. Each had their own ideas about that.

As they drove back to the hotel from the beach, Shannon posed the first question. "When are you going back to Washington?"

"I don't know. There's nothing I have to do there right now."

Tony had left Sam with a neighbor, so he didn't worry about him.

"Do you like cruises?"

Tony had to pretend he did. "Well of course, if the weather is good."

"There's one leaving to Hawaii tomorrow night. Fifteen days round trip! Are you interested?"

Tony clearly believed he was in a state of grace now. He smiled at her, squeezed her hand and replied. "That would be perfect."

Excited, Shannon took out her iPad and made a reservation. "But I insist on paying my half. It was my suggestion."

"How much is it?" he said, trying not to care.

"$4200, but that includes lodging in Maui." Shannon was buoyant.

"No, I'll take care of it." He pulled out a credit card so she could confirm the trip.

"But that's $8400 total. Are you sure?"

Ugh. She meant $4200 per person, double occupancy. Those damn cruise ads. He swallowed a mouthful of Coke Zero from the can in his cup holder.

"No worries. Book it."

Shannon finished the reservation and snuggled next to Tony. "Thanks lover. I'm going to make this a cruise you'll never forget."

Tony wasn't likely to forget. Visa would make sure of that. What was he thinking? Oh yes, of course.

"I'll need to buy a few things before we leave. What about you? Are you packed for two weeks in paradise?" She emphasized 'paradise' as she rubbed his thigh.

"Yes, I'll need some more clothes too. What time do we sail?"

"Seven at night. We can shop in the morning, return your rental car and take a cab to the dock."

So they spent their last night at the Grand Californian, a repetition of the first three, lovemaking in the late afternoon, dinner, more lovemaking, then sleep, only to be woken at 2:00am for another tumble. Not that Tony was complaining. He hadn't had this much in many years.

***

They arrived at the dock at 5:30pm with new luggage, clothing and outlook. They were now officially a couple, on a romantic cruise, with all the expectations that implies. It would either be paradise or a disaster, depending on how they got along. After all, they had just met and sometimes you discover incompatibilities in confined passage.

Remember, Tony thought Shannon was a wealthy woman in her thirties who had just sold her company. Shannon thought Tony was a wealthy man in his fifties. But Tony was living off the $500,000 he got from selling his shack on the harbor. God Bless America. Essentially, Tony and Shannon had reinvented themselves and neither wanted the truth to come out anytime soon.

Tony knew what he had to do. Eat right, take extra vitamins and exercise daily, in order to survive, uh satisfy, his new lover. Shannon had similar plans, but it included setting up romantic opportunities on the boat and particularly in the cabin.

Before walking up the entrance to the boat, Shannon turned to Tony, threw her arms around him and gave him a long, passionate kiss.

"I hope you're ready."

Tony hoped so too. He smiled. "I am."

Hand in hand, they walked up the plank to the boat, found their cabin and settled in. Or so Tony thought. Their bags had already been placed in the room, and the table was decorated with flowers, fruit, champagne and chocolate. Shannon walked sensually over to Tony and began to undress him.

"Don't we have a reception tonight?"

Shannon continued to undress him, then started to undress herself.

"We can be a little late. I can't wait that long for you."

An hour later, they were getting ready for the Captain's reception and dinner at 7:30. The horns sounded as the boat left the dock. The moon was out and people were waiving good-bye from the shore.

After a lavish reception with gourmet food and tropical drinks, the couple returned to their cabin for, well, you can guess. Tony wished he really was 57 now.

"Shannon, you're going to wear me out," he said with a smile.

"How did you guess?" she said seductively. They were both sound asleep by midnight.

Shannon woke Tony up before sunrise. He was half asleep and not ready for her yet.

"Can we sleep a little more first dear?"

"Not that silly. I want to watch the sun rise. Get up, it's almost time."

Tony and Shannon, wearing robes over their sleepwear, put on flip-flops and walked out to view the sunrise. It was cool. Fog covered the boat. It reminded him of his walks at home, but Gig Harbor was nothing like this.

"Oh, there it is. Isn't is beautiful Tony?"

"Lovely. Can we go back to bed now?"

"Of course lover, what was I thinking?"

Shannon led him back to the room, began undressing him for the morning romp. Apparently the sunrise excited her, not that he was complaining. He just thought they might sleep in today, but didn't protest.

"You first lover" she said as she prepared him for mounting.

Nope. Not this morning. Maybe another day.

The couple spent the next nine days loving and living together as a couple. There were side trips to islands, special nights with those tropical shows where they throw flame torches around and roast a pig in the ground, all accompanied by native Hawaiian music. They bought souvenirs and clothing at local shops. It was almost as if this was a honeymoon, although it was largely indistinguishable to anyone seeing them.

But on the last day in Maui, the weather changed completely. An earthquake and typhoon in the South Pacific was causing massive waves heading to the Hawaiian Islands. Storm surges swamped the waterfront hotels and prevented cruise ships from leaving. Power lines and trees were falling and electricity was going out. The cruise passengers were told they could stay on the ship or on land. About half of the passengers chose to stay on the ship, including Tony and Shannon.

A ship at sea can take an alternate course, away from storms. But a ship in port cannot, it is confined with the local weather conditions.

The cruise director made the most of the inclement weather, providing fun activities for the guests, even a murder mystery dinner that night. Shannon wanted to participate in the show, as some of the guests could join the detective in solving the crime. She pulled Tony in as well, who reluctantly agreed. With help from some Hollywood movie passengers, the mystery was both exciting and realistic.

"Ladies and gentlemen. My name is Inspector Robinson. I gathered you here to determine who might have killed Jonathan Williams, a carpenter from nearby Leeds. We need to search for clues that will lead us to the killer. Officer Hempstead has found some already."

Shannon nudged Tony, who wore a Sherlock Holmes style hat. All the guests participating wore hats to distinguish them from the other passengers. Shannon wore an Irish Flat Cap and a tartan tie.

"Isn't this great Tony? Maybe we'll find the clue that solves the mystery."

"Let's hope so dear. Otherwise, it might be a long night."

"Officer Hempstead, tell the other detectives what you have found."

"Of course inspector. Here is a bullet casing, from a handgun. It held a 45-caliber size bullet. And in this bag is a substance that was found next to the casing, some sort of material we believe came off the shoe of the killer. Finally, we have some blood drops that led from the casing to that door."

Officer Hempstead pointed to a door in the ballroom.

"Unfortunately, we don't have a body. It must have been moved. And, we don't have the equipment required to test the blood or test for prints or DNA from the bullet casing. That will have to wait until we make port. But we believe that with more clues we can identify the killer and secure him, so he can't murder anyone else. Will you help me look for more clues?"

The guests cheered the bobby on and were ready to search.

"Very well then. Spread out around the ship and look for anything that might be suspicious. Use the gloves we gave you and place any evidence in the plastic bags you have. You don't want your DNA or prints to get on evidence, do you?"

"Not bloody likely", said one of the guest detectives. The room laughed.

"Very well then. And remember one more point. There is still a murderer loose on the ship, so be careful where you go."

The guest detectives moved out of the ballroom and to various points on the ship. Tony and Shannon decided to start with the recreation room at the stern of the ship. It was raining heavily so the clues must have been placed inside the ship, not on outer decks.

"What do you think we're looking for Tony?"

"I don't know. Guess we'll know if we find anything."

Shannon looked in a large plastic box, which held the volleyballs, nets and other sports equipment. Pushing aside the yellow spheres, she saw something. "Tony, I think I see the gun."

Tony reached down and saw a gun. Using his gloves, he lifted it up to his nose.

"It doesn't smell like it's been fired."

Tony put the weapon into one of the evidence bags. Shannon couldn't wait to show the others.

"This must be a major clue. Oh, I'm so excited. Maybe we'll win the free cruise for solving the murder."

Tony loved the youthful exuberance Shannon showered on him. It was nice to have someone not preoccupied with their health or finances, the topics that dominate older people.

"That's great Shannon. Let's bring it back right away."

Tony and Shannon headed back to the ballroom. Suddenly, there was a flash of lightning and a crack of thunder. It was deafening, so it must have been right on top of the ship. The lights went out; small emergency lights from the floor came on.

"Do you think this is part of the game?"

"Maybe. Let's use your cell phone so we can read the signs that lead back to the ballroom."

Before they had gone ten steps, another loud noise. This was clearly a gunshot and it sounded close. Shannon hugged Tony.

"Tony, I'm scared."

"I'm a little scared myself. Just hold onto me and we'll get back to the others."

They walked hand in hand, Shannon holding her cell phone looking for directional signs. They couldn't remember how they got to the recreation room because there were too many turns, and three flights of stairs below the ballroom.

As they were walking up the first flight of stairs, Shannon held her phone's light in front of her face, so she could find the next turn. Then she screamed.

"Tony. Look."

It was a body and it didn't look like it was part of the game. Blood continued to ooze from the man's forehead, but he was clearly dead. Shannon averted her eyes and held Tony tight.

"What do we do? Tony, someone was really murdered here tonight."

Tony was trying to hold himself together, for her sake. But he was shivering and panicked as well.

"Take a picture with your phone. Then let's keep going."

Shannon took a picture then scurried around the body, pulling Tony with her. She continued crying and muttering about the body.

"This isn't fun Tony. I wish we had stayed on land."

"We'll get through this dear. We just have to get back to the others. That looks like the second flight of stairs we have to take."

Just then one of the stateroom doors opened and a man with a gun hustled them inside.

"Be quiet and you won't get hurt."

Tony and Shannon wanted to scream, but dared not. Once they were inside the stateroom, the man zip tied them together. Shannon was at the point of fainting and Tony couldn't help her.

"Well, I guess you found the killer. Congratulations. Did you find the body too?"

Tony and Shannon looked at each other. This man was smiling and not in a killer sort of way.

"We found a body downstairs. Is that where you killed him?"

The man took out an ID card, with the word KILLER on it.

"No friends. I'm the killer from the murder mystery. You solved the crime. Now let me untie you."

"Wait, we heard a gunshot and saw a man shot in the forehead. That wasn't the body."

The man looked panicked now.

"No, the fake body was in the recreation room, in a closet next to the equipment."

The man took out a walkie-talkie.

"This is Johnson. Two of the guests found me so the game is over. But they saw another body not far from here, a real one. Send the police!"

A panicked response came back.

"The only police are on the island. We'll have to wait for them. Lock yourselves in the stateroom and wait until we can come get you."

"Folks, it looks like we'll have to stay here and be quiet. There's a real murderer out there."

Tony and Shannon huddled on the bed, leaving the man to guard the door.

"Is your gun real?"

"No, but maybe it will fool someone coming through the door."

Shannon curled herself in Tony's arms and began crying. "Tony, I'm scared. What if the killer finds us?"

"I'll protect you dear. We'll get through this."

Thirty minutes later the man got another message on his walkie-talkie.

"All right Johnson. The cops are here and have apprehended the suspect. You can bring your heroes back to the ballroom."

Tony and Shannon heaved a sigh of relief. Lights in the stateroom came back on.

"Good, the power has returned. I'll bring you back to the ballroom."

Up another stairway and a few more turns, they entered the last door to the ballroom. As it opened, they were greeted by cheering and laughter. Flying confetti and balloons were everywhere. All the guests had smiles on their faces. The inspector welcomed them in.

"Congratulations Tony and Shannon. You solved the crime and found the suspect."

Tony was still confused. Shannon hadn't stopped shaking.

"But what about the real murder?"

The inspector continued.

"No real murder. That body you found came from our friends in Hollywood, several of them were on the ship scouting a location for a movie. Looked real, didn't it?"

Tony and Shannon finally relaxed.

"Now, here is your voucher for an all expenses cruise you can use in the next year. Congratulations!"

The big band started to play dance music and everyone joined in, as if it was New Year's Eve and the year had just changed. Waiters brought food and drinks for everyone.

Tony and Shannon had seats of honor near the band. They had a late dinner, and danced a few times. Tony looked at Shannon's face, her makeup now mussed from the crying.

"Had enough excitement for one night dear?"

"Yes, but the night isn't over yet." She took him by the hand back to their stateroom.

As they arrived, they heard an announcement on the intercom.

"You'll be glad to know that the storm will be moving through the area tonight and we should be able to leave for the mainland tomorrow."

Shannon was more assertive than usual that night, probably to extricate the fear she endured. Feeling very close and safe with Tony, she was particularly verbal during sex.

"Take me Tony. Oh, take me. That's it. Yes!"

Shannon moaned and described every feeling she had. As she was reaching orgasm, she dug her red polished fingernails into Tony's back, thrust her body up and down and let out a cry men know only as good news. But then, an unexpected utterance.

"I love you Tony. I love you."

Under the circumstances, there is only one thing the man has to do.

"I love you too Shannon."

They collapsed holding each other and then fell asleep. After a bit, Tony got up to go to the bathroom. He returned to find Shannon sound asleep. They didn't wake until 9:00am. Tony finally got to sleep in. Shannon was the first to get up.

Tony had recovered from the drama and intense lovemaking they had last night. Shannon kept full eye contact with him as they made love now. She was clearly a woman in love. It made it even more exciting for him too. But this time was fast. She reached orgasm quickly just as she had brought him to climax. When they were done, she shook her long hair around, planted a kiss on him and hopped off.

"Let's go lover. I'm starving."

They showered, dressed and were at the breakfast buffet within 30 minutes. While they were eating, the boat horn began to blow, signifying that they would depart within the hour. Guests that stayed on the island were scurrying back to the ship.

Both Tony and Shannon had secrets they were keeping from the other, but they didn't know that the other person had a secret as well. They were only three days out from the L.A. port now, so there wasn't much time to come clean.

It was eerie how well they got along, even though the relationship was built on fiction. It was almost three weeks now of idyllic love, food and wine. Like the commercials you don't believe. Was she telling him the truth? Why would she settle for someone his age when she could obviously find someone in his thirties? What would happen when they got back to L.A.? Tony needed a plan.

Then Tony remembered dropping the 'L' word. It was only in response to her sexually charged use of it at the height of mutual orgasm. He didn't mean it, but what could he do now? You can't take it back, not to a woman who says it first.

Shannon was also worried. Should she tell Tony the truth, how she wasn't wealthy, how she spent most of her money already and had only a small apartment in the desert to return to. Why would Tony want to stay with her if he knew? He could easily find someone of substance, someone really in her thirties, and with money. Shannon needed a plan.

She decided she would tell Tony the truth. It might lead to the end of their relationship, but she couldn't keep lying. Lies always come out, sooner or later.

For a moment, Tony thought of Sam, so he called his neighbor Joe who was watching him.

"Tony, I was hoping you would call."

"I've been busy Joe. How is Sam?"

"I'm sorry Tony. Sam passed away a few days ago. Never woke up. I'm sure he went peacefully."

Tony sighed and let out a little tear. "Joe, can you..."

"I already took care of him. The vet laid him to rest in a small pet burial plot. You'll be able to visit him when you get back."

"Thanks Joe. I'll call you when I get back."

"One more thing Tony. You got two calls, one from a lawyer and one from a realtor. You really ought to get a cell phone. Here's are the numbers."

Tony called the lawyer first. Apparently, his wife had an insurance policy she bought that Tony didn't know about. $100,000. The lawyer said he would wire it to Tony's bank.

Then he called the realtor. A development company wanted to put up condos overlooking the harbor. The ten acres they needed included his little quarter-acre lot and 1000sf house. They offered him $400,000.

Shannon came into the stateroom and saw Tony crying.

"What's wrong dear?"

"Oh, an old friend died."

"What was his name?"

"Sam. We've been friends for 18 years."

Shannon comforted Tony. "I'm sorry to hear that. Did Sam work for your company?"

"No, just someone I spent time with."

Sam's death and the two financial windfalls gave Tony an upset stomach. His mixed emotions, along with his worry about the truth coming out to Shannon became too much. He hadn't told Shannon that Sam was his dog, or anything about the new money. The lies were starting to pile up.

"Shannon. Do they sell phones on the boat?"

"Yes, they have cell phones in the ship store, why?"

"Well, I left mine at home and I'm due for a new one."

Tony never had a cell phone.

"To tell you the truth, I haven't used mine much since we met. No one else I wanted to get in touch with. But it sure was handy during the murder mystery."

Shannon didn't think this was the best time to tell Tony about her situation, seeing that a good friend had just passed away. She would wait until later.

Tony started up his new iPhone.

"May I have your number dear?" They laughed. Their relationship started with sex and was about to end with exchanging phone numbers.

"Yes, I hope you'll call me sometime."

"Tony, I have a confession."

"Yes dear. What is it?"

"I'm not wealthy. My business was just some honeybee hive. I sold them to a company for a few thousand dollars. I don't live in San Diego; I live in an apartment in Dulzura? And I sold my car to raise some money to come here. I was hoping to meet someone and I met you."

"That's all right. I'm lucky to have met you too."

"And I'm not 36, I'm 43."

"Is that all?"

Shannon sighed some relief but was clearly upset.

"Yes, so now you know. Guess this is the end of our time together."

Tony took her face in his hands and kissed her.

"Not if I have anything to say about it."

Tony didn't take this opportunity to tell his side of the story. Maybe he could get to it later.

Their lovemaking that night was just as intense, but even more authentic than before. Shannon was feeling very secure now. She had unburdened herself and Tony still wanted to be with her.

Tony was also feeling secure. With close to a million dollars in the bank, thanks to the unexpected life insurance policy, and sale of his home and business, Tony didn't think he needed to ruin a good thing with the truth. And now he had a cell phone.

There were still a couple pitfalls he had to worry about. Shannon expected that he lived in some fancy house in Gig Harbor and what about his car, a 1994 Volvo with 250,000 miles on it. Not exactly the Corvette she had been used to.

They were eating breakfast on the deck. The sun was shining. They needed a plan.

"Shannon dear?"

"Yes love."

"What are you doing for Thanksgiving?"

"No plans really. My boy is in the service and won't be home this year."

"How would you like to go to Boston?"

"Oh, I would love that. I've never been there."

"My daughter and her family live there, on the ocean. And the autumn colors are wonderful."

"That's great, but I'll need some clothing suitable for the weather. I only have Socal digs."

"Me too. How does this sound? We'll fly to Boston for Thanksgiving with my daughter, then get a car and drive to Florida, where we can take that cruise we won."

"That's so great Tony. I'm so glad we're going to do that." Shannon was excited.

Tony called Joe.

"Joe, this is Tony. Please go to my house and give all my stuff to charity. Take anything you like, including the car. I'll pay for any expenses you have. The developers will be knocking down the house next month."

"Thanks Tony. Even your record collection?"

"Sure thing. I'm going to buy them again on CDs."

"And to think, I knew you before you were rich and famous."

"Not rich or famous. You're still my good friend."

"OK Tony, I'll take care of it."

The next day the ship docked in L.A.

**

Just as they planned, Tony and Shannon went shopping for some cold weather clothing, and then took a plane to Boston, to have Thanksgiving with his daughter.

Tony splurged for first class tickets.

"I've never been in first class Tony. This is so nice."

"Well, after a while, you can't go back to coach."

Tony was still spinning the lie.

The flight attendants pampered them, especially Shannon. Champagne, fresh fruit, gourmet meal, choice of 3 wines, fresh warm cookies, hot washcloth, the works. It was a non-stop flight to Boston and Shannon fell asleep after the meal.

Tony figured out how to check his bank balance on the iPhone. Hmm. With the new money from the life insurance and the house sale, his balance was $980,982. And that's after paying for the cruise. He didn't have a car or a place to live, but he was doing all right.

The flight attendant put a blanket on Shannon and turned off the lights. Tony pushed his seat back as well and snuggled next to his new girl. His new girl, just like a teenager.

He had a little talk with his daughter, in order to keep up appearances with Shannon. They agreed not to talk about money or his previous circumstances. Even the granddaughter played along with the game – Papa Tony made some money.

Two hours out of Boston now. A BMW would be waiting for them at Logan Airport, which he had already purchased on line. Aren't smart phones wonderful? It was new, but just the low-end model, seating for four and a large trunk. It was the perfect vehicle for a couple on a romantic road trip.

Shannon woke up, asking for tea and those cookies.

"Well, you had a nice nap."

"This seat is more comfortable than my bed. Tony, you've been so good to me."

Tony smiled. "We've been good for each other." All the pampering really had an effect on Shannon. She did look 36, after all. Money, comfort and love will do that for a woman. Now he wished he had told his daughter how old Shannon was. It didn't come up. Good thing they were staying at a hotel instead of their house.

Maybe this would be a good time to tell Shannon the truth? Then we wouldn't have to pretend at Thanksgiving. No, this isn't the right time. Maybe later.

They collected their bags and met the BMW sales rep, just as promised. He put the bags in the trunk, opened the car door for Shannon, and then gave Tony the keys and registration.

"Wow. This car is beautiful." She leaned over to kiss him. "And I can reach you from here." Tony wondered what she meant.

"We have to stop in Boston for dessert. I want to surprise them with some good Italian pastry from the North End. You won't believe how good it is."

"Can we get some flowers for your daughter and maybe something for your granddaughter?"

"Of course. Why don't you think of something for a 7 year old girl."

They picked up flowers at Quincy Market and pastries from Mike's; then they headed up 1A toward Manchester, a very exclusive town. Tony's daughter married well, a doctor and so she was a stay at home mom.

He was a gentleman, never talking down to Tony, treating him with respect. Tony raised his daughter right and it showed in the type of man she chose to marry.

Meanwhile, Shannon was on her iPad looking for gifts. She found a Calafant Princess Castle that you build and color and showed it to Tony.

"Oh, she'll love that. There's a toy store on the way."

It was the Wednesday before Thanksgiving and they were arriving for dinner. They pulled into the driveway, a relatively modest house, but right on the ocean.

"Pop, I'm so glad you're here. How have you been?" said his daughter Maria. They hugged.

"I'm good Maria. I'm glad to be here. This is my friend Shannon." Shannon hugged Maria and gave her the flowers.

"Nice to meet you Shannon." She gave Tony a look (you didn't say you were dating a younger woman).

"Thank you, they're beautiful. Come inside." Maria's daughter Olivia ran to her grandfather.

"Papa Tony. I love you."

"I love you too sweetheart. My friend Shannon brought you a present."

Olivia looked at the box and gave a little scream. "A princess castle with crayons. This is great." She gave Shannon a hug, and then she ran off to open it.

"Tony, good to see you. Hi, I'm Mike, Maria's husband. I'm glad you could come for the holiday."

They all went inside for drinks and chatter.

"Dinner will be ready in an hour Pop. Shannon, would you mind helping Olivia with the castle?"

"I'd be glad to. C'mon Olivia, where can we start this?"

Olivia took Shannon to her playroom and they started making the castle. Maria snuck back into the living room.

"Pop, isn't she kind of young for you?"

"Maria, she makes me happy."

"I can see why. And flexible too, I'll bet."

"Now, don't embarrass me. I was faithful to your mother all my life, but I was very lonely this last year."

"Nothing wrong with starting over Tony. Maria, don't give your dad a hard time."

"I'm just kidding with him. How old is she Pop?"

"Stop it. You'll just have to wonder." Mike changed the subject.

"Are you taking care of yourself, still walking, seeing your doctor?"

"Yes Mike, thanks. I feel fine and I'm walking four miles a day around town."

"Good, we want you around for Olivia's wedding."

"If I possibly can, I'll be there."

"If he stays with Shannon, he might outlive us all."

Dinner was casual and went just as Tony had planned. No awkward conversation. After dinner, Olivia went back to work on her castle and the adults had tea and dessert in the family room.

"The Celtics are on at eight. Tony, you want to watch with me?"

"Oh Mike, he probably wants to get to the hotel with Shannon; don't make him stay up here all night."

"No Maria, that's all right. I'd like to take Shannon for a walk on singing beach, but then I'll watch the first half with you."

"It's a deal. Wear your jacket, it's windy out there."

"I remember."

"Why is it called singing beach?" said Shannon.

"Well, if you're in your bare feet, the sand squeaks as you walk."

"Really?"

"Yes, you'll see."

"It's true Shannon. No beach like it anywhere."

Tony and Shannon went for their walk. Mike helped Maria clean up.

"It good for your dad to have a companion. That will keep him healthy."

"I know dear. How healthy?"

"Stop it. She's probably in her forties."

"Maybe, and Pop is 64. There's more than years difference, there's energy and, you know."

"That's probably why he's seeing her. You're 35 now, right?"

Maria threw a towel at Mike. "I'll show you how old I am, dear."

Meanwhile on the beach, Shannon was awestruck by the ocean's horizon and stars coming out.

"Tony, this must be the best place to live on Earth."

"It's not bad, but way out of my budget."

"I'd be happy with you anywhere, except Dulzura that is."

They both laughed. "OK, we won't live there, but that leaves a lot of country."

"We better get back. You promised Mike you would watch the game with him."

"OK. But just the first half. I want to get to the hotel."

Tony and Mike watched the Celtics for an hour while Maria and Shannon got to know each other better.

"How they look this year Mike?"

"Well, it's not 1986, but they'll make the playoffs."

"Good, as long as they do, it's a good year. And the Bruins?"

"Sorry to tell you it's another rebuilding year after making the playoffs for 24 years straight."

"Seems unholy somehow."

"Yes, I understand the arch bishop is on the phone to the Pope."

They laughed. The women could hear them.

"Tony loves Mike. He was so happy when we married."

"I can see why. He's really perfect."

"Not perfect, but close."

Olivia called from her room.

"Mommy, I'm going to bed now."

"Good girl. I'll be up in a minute to tuck you in."

"She puts herself to bed? What are you feeding that child?"

"What can I say? I have the perfect husband and daughter."

Tony and Shannon said goodnight and headed downtown to the hotel. Mike questioned Maria.

"You were polite with Shannon, weren't you?"

"She's great. Just what my father needed."

"And you're just what I need. Now get your pretty butt upstairs and I'll show you how young you are."

Manchester had a quaint bed and breakfast above an Irish bar and restaurant. Tony and Shannon checked in, and then went downstairs for a nightcap.

"What do you think?"

"It's great Tony. What a lovely room and bar. How long are we staying?"

"Just a couple days. First we'll see a little of Boston, and then we head to NYC for two nights, see a Broadway show and some tourist sites."

"Sounds like a dream come true."

Tony and Shannon listened to some live Irish music, had their drinks and went up to bed. It had been a very family day, bringing Tony and Shannon closer together.

In the morning, the fog covered most of downtown Manchester and out to the beach.

"Tony, isn't the fog romantic?"

"Yes, I love the fog."

Fog used to depress Tony, but he could see now it was all a matter of one's circumstances. Fog could be depressing, but it could also be romantic.

Tony and Shannon made love in the morning, and then headed over to Maria's house for Thanksgiving. It was a perfect day. Maria, Mike and Olivia welcomed Shannon as if she was part of the family. Tony and Mike watched football while Shannon helped Maria with dinner. Olivia worked on her castle, coloring each part with care.

At the dinner table, Mike prayed for everyone's good health and thanks for bringing Tony and Shannon to their home. He concluded with a travel request.

"Please look after Tony and Shannon as the drive to Florida. Grant them good weather and safe travel."

"Thank you Mike", said Shannon.

After dinner Tony and Shannon walked the beach again, the sand squeaking beneath their toes.

***

Tony and Shannon had a dream road trip down the coast. First they explored Boston and its historical sites, and then they stopped in NYC for Broadway shows and fine dining. Next, they went to Philadelphia, had cheese steaks and went to a Flyer's game. They topped off the whirlwind with time in Washington, D.C., and sightseeing of the national monuments. By this time, both were fully committed to each other. Shannon's "I love you" utterance that Tony reluctantly replied, was now a fact of their lives. Tony had even thought of asking Shannon to marry him. That would come to light later in the trip, in a most extraordinary way.

Walt Disney World is the stop for couples in love; many choose it for weddings and honeymoons. Tony and Shannon's time there was more like a couple celebrating their tenth wedding anniversary, even though it had only been months since they first met.

The weeklong stay was followed by a cruise, which they had won solving the murder mystery. This cruise would take them around the Caribbean with stops on exotic islands, the perfect place for Tony's proposal. He had slipped away from her just long enough to purchase a $10,000 engagement ring that he tucked away for the right moment.

Their lovemaking hadn't subsided a bit, since that night they exchanged I love you's. In fact, it had become so intense that Tony was considering a visit to the doctor for a checkup. The fog of Gig Harbor was so distant in his mind; he wondered what God was bestowing on him, this one hundred and eighty degree turn in life. He must have done something right in his 64 years.

Walking hand in hand on Cayman Island, they found a jungle path with exotic birds, colorful plants and luscious fruits hanging from trees. The sounds of monkeys, parrots and insects accented the surroundings.

"Shannon, what do you think of all these colors?"

"I've seen pictures and nature shows on television, but it is much more fantastic in person. Even the cruise ads aren't this beautiful."

"You know what else might make this a special experience?"

"What dear?"

Shannon was eager to hear the next words. She had fallen in love with Tony.

Tony pulled the ring box out of his pocket and then knelt down in front of Shannon.

"Shannon, you've been so good to me. Your love has filled me with more than I ever deserved. I can't think of anyone else I would rather spend the rest of my life with. Shannon Erin O'Toole, would you make me the happiest...."

Suddenly, two men dressed in white with black ski masks came out of the woods, grabbed Tony and disappeared just as quickly. Shannon screamed and chased them but one of the men sent her back with a wave of a gun. She was frantic and ran back to the town to get help.

Two hours later, Shannon's cell phone rang. It was Tony, or at least Tony's phone.

"We have your husband. We want $5,000,000 in small bills; put it in a duffel bag by tomorrow. Wait for further instructions."

"We don't have $5,000,000. Or at least I don't have access to it."

"This is the Cayman Islands, my dear. You can just go into town and get it."

"But I don't know anything about his accounts. You would have to ask him."

"We have, but he denies having an account. For his sake, I hope you can convince him to tell you."

"Can I speak with him?"

"Here he is."

"Tony, are you OK?"

"Shannon, I'm OK for now, but they think I'm some millionaire with hidden cash in the Cayman Islands."

"But that's what I thought too."

"Shannon, I hate to say this, especially under these circumstances. I haven't told you the truth about my life or possessions."

"What do you mean?"

"Well, I've never been wealthy. I've never been to college. I just happened to have a small shanty on the harbor that a hotel wanted to buy for the land. And a developer wanted to build condos on land that I had a tiny house on. Both the hotel and developer gave me a lot of money to sell. My house has been knocked down. I gave my old car to a friend who was watching my dog while we were in Socal. Worst of all, my daughter has been playing along, just so I wouldn't have to tell you the truth."

"Is that all?"

"Isn't that enough?"

"Did you really have a friend named Sam that died?"

"Actually, Sam was my dog. He died while my friend Joe was watching him."

"I see. Why didn't you tell me the truth? Didn't you think I could understand?"

"I meant to tell you. I really did. I'm so sorry. If I ever see you again, I'll never lie to you again."

Shannon started to cry, realizing that Tony's lie may cost him his life.

"Please let me talk to them. I'll convince them that you don't have the money."

Tony put the kidnappers back on the phone with Shannon.

"Listen. Tony's been telling you the truth. He doesn't have $5,000,000 in some Cayman Islands bank. He doesn't have that kind of money at all."

"We saw the ring he was giving you. We know he has money. We'll drop the demand to $3,000,000, but it better be here by tomorrow at noon. We will call with instructions then."

Shannon heard the kidnappers hang up and started to cry. She went back to town and told the police. They told her this sort of kidnapping is common in the islands, particularly with wealthy people. When she explained that Tony wasn't wealthy and didn't have the money, they shrugged and sighed.

"We'll do our best."

Shannon cried even harder, realizing the police would have to be very lucky to help her. As she walked out of the police station, a man came up to her.

"What is the trouble?"

"My boyfriend has been kidnapped and they are asking for more money than we can come up with."

"Maybe I can help. Tell me all the details. And I'll need a picture of your boyfriend."

Shannon recounted the details and gave the man a picture of Tony she had on her phone. The man took her phone number and said he would get back to her in the morning.

Shannon didn't hear from the kidnappers and couldn't call them. She hardly slept at all, in her cabin on the ship. The next morning her phone rang. It was the man who offered to help.

"Miss O'Toole?"

"Yes."

"Meet me at this address around 11:30 this morning."

"All right. Do you have a way we can get Tony back?"

"We hope so. Meet me there promptly."

Shannon met the mysterious stranger as requested. He took her phone and hooked it to some computer looking device with an antenna.

"When the kidnappers call back, you'll talk to them. Say you have the money, but you can't drop it off until 1:00pm. They will agree and give you an address."

Shannon did exactly as directed. The kidnappers called, accepted the offer for 1:00pm and gave her a location to drop off the money. Meanwhile, the device with her phone captured the location of the kidnappers.

"What do I do now?"

"Nothing. Go back to the ship and wait. I'll call you when I have news."

One o'clock came and went. There were no more calls to Shannon's phone from the kidnappers. She was frantic and feeling helpless. Then her phone rang.

"Miss O'Toole, can you please come outside to the deck facing the dock?"

Shannon came out and looked to the dock. There was Tony running up the ship's plank to join her. The mysterious stranger was nowhere in sight. Shannon jumped into Tony's arms.

"Darling, I thought you would be killed."

"I thought I would never see you again."

"Are you hurt Tony?"

"No. Two men in military clothing killed the kidnappers and brought me here. I never even saw their faces."

"Who do you think they were?"

"CIA, mercenaries, I don't know and I don't care. I just wish I had given you that ring earlier. The kidnappers took it."

They returned to their cabin to get over the trauma. Tony was physically fine, just rattled from the danger. Later, they had an early dinner and planned to go to bed early. Someone knocked on the cabin door. Shannon opened it.

"Yes, may I help you?"

"A delivery ma'am."

Shannon took the package and read the label.

To: Mr. and Mrs. Tony Granelli
The cruise line wishes you a fantastic honeymoon!
From: Captain Johnson

Tony and Shannon looked at each other, wondering what this was about. They opened the large envelope. Inside was an envelope with a voucher for a two-week cruise, all expenses paid, by the cruise line, to make up for their traumatic experience.

"Honeymoon?" Tony reached into the envelope. There was another small felt bag. Inside was the engagement ring he had bought for Shannon.

Dream a Little Dream

Have you ever had a great dream and were sad when you woke up because the dream was over? That happened to Joe last week. In the dream, Joe was back in high school and was very popular; this was very different from his real life high school experience. All the prettiest girls wanted to be around him; he found himself dating Connie, the prettiest girl in his class. They made out for hours in the backseat of his mustang convertible at the drive-in.

Why couldn't he have this dream every night? If only he could start every day with this dream, the life he never had when he was 17. He would be so happy. Can you order up a dream?

Joe wished he could have Connie forever, if only in his dreams. He did some research. Apparently, there were studies that indicated you could increase your chances of having a specific, desirable dream. It's called lucid dreaming. Some of the recommendations were:

- Go to sleep an hour earlier
- Control your diet
- Tackle stress
- Have a relaxing bedtime routine
- Put roses in your bedroom

Joe tried each one, even putting roses in his bedroom. But he was unable to recreate the dream with Connie. He wrote a long love letter to her and read it before sleeping. He put a picture of her from the yearbook on his nightstand. It was the one of her on the baton team. Her long blond hair framed her lovely face and beautiful smile. He thought about the one date he had with her, when he took her to the movies, but was too shy to do much more than an awkward kiss when he dropped her off. She was out of his league.

Joe had studied chemistry in college and worked in a pharmaceutical lab. He often wondered if they could create a pill that would allow people to have those lucid dreams. That would have to be a future discovery. We're still waiting for those flying cars we saw on the *Jetsons* and in *Back to the Future*.

That's where he met his wife Barbara; they had a boy and girl and in due course three grandchildren. Holidays and birthdays gave them many years of bliss. He realized that his family was his greatest source of happiness.

His family was also there for him when his wife passed away, naturally and peacefully in her sleep at the age of 60. She left him much too soon. He spent his retirement years fishing and reading. He remembered her packing a cooler for him to take on his small boat. When he returned with his catch, she would make it for dinner, as long as he cleaned it first. Now he would spend his nights reading by the fireplace, remembering the good times they had together.

He received an invitation to his high school reunion. At first, he didn't want to go, but later decided it would be better to be with old friends than to stay home alone. He even wore his soccer letter sweater, and it still fit!

It was a warm night in May. Some of his classmates still drove cars from the 60s, a Pontiac GTO, a Dodge Charger and a few Mustangs. This jogged pleasant memories of cruising on a date. He saw his classmates entering the school gym, dressed like they did in high school. They wore bell-bottom jeans and tie-dye shirts; the girls had long straight hair with flowers. Several guys wore wigs.

The theme was "man on the moon" as this was the class of 1969. The gym was decorated in space memorabilia; there were pictures of the crew and video of that famous moon landing. Music completed the picture. Sly and the Family Stone, the Beatles, the Rolling Stones, the Turtles and the Doors. It felt like 1969 again.

Then Joe saw her. The girl that got away. Connie's eyes looked lovingly at Joe; he pulled her close to him. They kissed, like he wishes they had back in high school.

"Connie, I've wanted you my whole life."

"Joe, I've wished for this too."

After dancing with each other all night, they left the reunion together. They made love like they were eighteen again. Hours of bliss, mutual orgasms and carefree loving. It was the hottest sex he ever had. He had finally fulfilled his life goal, to have Connie forever. His only regret was that this happened so late in life. But it's better to have your best love late, than not at all.

***

"Mr. Mariani."

"Yes?"

"Your father's cremation is done. We just need a signature for his new columbarium. This plaque will honor his final resting place. May I ask a personal question for the service?"

"Of course."

"Did he have any final wishes?"

"Well, we found him in his chair by the fire holding an invitation to his high school reunion. I know he really wanted to go and reconnect with an old girlfriend."

"Perhaps he was dreaming about it when he passed on."

"Yes, that would be a nice way to go."

"Thank you for choosing Clifford Scott Mortuary for his final home."

Who Stole Asbury Park?

In the halcyon days of 1964, when simple love songs played on pocket radios and boys turn their thoughts to girls and their first kiss, Tony was in the hullabaloo on the Asbury Park boardwalk, with the other eleven year old boys, watching the girls dance to the sounds of The Beatles, Beach Boys and The Four Seasons. Every so often a girl would come over and take a boy by the hand onto the dance floor while the rest of them tapped their feet, nodded to each other and wondered when some girl would rescue them from the wall. It was too risky to ask a girl to dance, but if they took the initiative, you were safe in the eyes of your buddies and there might even be a slow dance, a chance to hold a girl close to you.

"There goes David, with Becky Johnson," said Tony. Becky had short, blonde hair, saddle shoes, knee socks and a plaid skirt. "She's a good dancer."

Tony's friend Bobby agreed. "Yeah, if you like dancing."

Tony nudged Bobby. "Yeah, if you like dancing."

Tony was hoping some girl would ask him to dance, but couldn't let on to his friend. "The music's good though" as they bounced with the beat.

"Yeah" said the other boys.

The girls, completely smitten with Beatles music, were dancing, mostly with each other while others talked and checked out the boys on the wall. As Tony and Bobby watched the girls dance, another girl walked over to them from the left. "Would you like to dance?" said a pretty Italian girl in bell-bottom jeans and a red Danskin top.

"Me," said Tony, not sure if she was talking to him or Bobby.

"Yes, my name is Angela."

"Sure I guess so. I'm Tony" and he walked out to the dance floor with Angela as *Twist and Shout* played from the speakers. She turned to him and smiled, then started to twist, the main dance style at the time and the only dance adolescent boys could do. Tony watched Angela and tried to match her while maintaining a serious expression. Angela could tell how nervous he was.

"That's good Tony" trying to coach a smile out of him. He relaxed his facial muscles a bit.

"I'm not a good dancer, sorry" as his sneakers squeaked on the wooden floor.

Angela smiled. "It's ok." Her movements were much more graceful and pretty. Tony noticed her long hair and bangs bobbing with the beat. The DJ smoothly changed the song to *A Hard Days Night*.

As Tony looked at Angela, his thoughts raced and before he knew it, a slow song came on; *Because* by The Dave Clark Five, another group from the British invasion. He wasn't prepared for this. Tony looked at Angela and she looked back. He clumsily tried to slow dance, but it didn't matter. They were close. Tony held Angela's chest close to his but left just enough space below the waist to hide his newly found excitement. He wondered if this would scare her away. His anxiety was answered after the song.

Angela took Tony's hand and walked toward the exit. Tony followed obediently, his heart quickening. He could feel that Angela was nervous too, her hand moist. As they were about to leave, Angela turned to Tony. "Can we go for a walk?"

"Sure" he said, trying to hide his own nervousness. "Where are we going?"

"Down the boardwalk. I like seeing the rides at night."

"Yeah, they're neat. Hey, would you like an ice cream?"

"OK, a twist please." Tony ordered two cones and the couple continued walking. Eating the ice cream replaced a lot of conversation, as both of them were entering a new part of their young lives. When they were finished, Tony took a napkin and wiped some ice cream from Angela's lip, then she closed her eyes. With all the confidence he could muster, he leaned in and kissed her. Angela put her arms around Tony and they kissed again.

"Do you want to walk on the beach?" she said.

"Sure" both of them smiling now.

They left their shoes under the boardwalk and walked barefoot near the water, Angela holding his hand tightly. Tony could smell her hair; it had a fruity scent, he wanted to tell her without sounding dumb.

"Your hair smells nice." Tony was starting to relax.

"Thanks. It's my shampoo. Strawberries."

"Neat. You dress nice too." Tony couldn't help glancing at her small breasts, curving through the top. He was thinking about kissing Angela again and hoped she was too.

"Thanks. I like your turtleneck." They walked up and down the beach, and then returned to get their shoes.

Angela gave Tony a look that he understood. They lay down in the sand under the boardwalk and spent the next hour kissing and holding each other closely. It was Tony's first make out session and probably Angela's too. These were the memories that last a lifetime, the first, awkward steps into love.

***

It was the summer of 2012 when Tony and his California wife Barbara, in town for a wedding, drove to Asbury Park, her first time on the Jersey shore and his visit reminding him of that magical night in 1964. He was surprised to find parking close to the beach. As they walked up the stairs onto the boardwalk, he noticed something odd. It was deserted; only a few people on the beach and the buildings that once held a carousel, stadium and dance hall were rusty, disintegrated and empty as if they had been bombed. Tony's dream memory fell flat.

"What the hell happened here?" he said.

"The beach is beautiful. Why isn't anyone here?"

"I don't know. This was such a great place when I was a kid. Let's get back in the car and go somewhere else."

As Tony drove, Barbara did some research on her phone. "I have it. The town went bankrupt back in the 90s and the city can't afford to bring back business. But they still charge $5 to go on the beach."

"Only in New Jersey could you have a beautiful beach and boardwalk and not make money. No one is on the beach because there aren't any bathrooms, food stands or anything else. We're not leaving until you see the real Jersey shore."

They drove up to Seaside Heights and parked. Walking up the steps to the boardwalk, they saw what Tony had been hoping for. "This is the real thing, Barbara." Thousands of young people filled the beach, boardwalk and restaurants. There were hundreds of painted, wooden buildings with all sorts of food, games and shops with cheap souvenirs. Barbara's eyes lit up when she heard music.

"Hey, look over here. There's a dance floor." She took Tony's hand and rushed them over to the music. *Can't Buy Me Love* came on. Tony and Barbara twisted like it was 1964. Tony thought of Angela as he danced with his wife.

Preheat the Microwave.Com

Instead of complaining about old people, Lisa decided to make lemonade. She got the idea during a visit to her grandmother. "Nana, what do you want for dinner?" she said.

"There's some chicken in the freezer, Lisa. That would be good." Nana filled a plastic measuring cup with water and put it in the microwave, set the timer to three minutes and pressed start.

"I can make your tea, Nana. You relax and watch your show."

Nana put her hand on Lisa's arm. "No dear. You have to preheat the microwave." Lisa paused silently, realizing that her grandmother was completely serious.

So Lisa made a deal with the maintenance guy to put hidden cameras and audio bugs in and around her Nana's elderly housing apartments, in the dining room, laundry room and in the elevator. They created an Internet site, *Preheat the Microwave.Com*. "Oh Mike, this will be so funny" she said touching his arm. If Lisa and Mike weren't married to others, this might have been the start of something. "These old timers never go on the Internet and we're not going to use any names. Besides, I checked with a lawyer and he said there's no problem."

Unit 204: "Where's the remote control?" said Sam.

"Here, eat your oatmeal dear," said his wife Alice.

"My show is coming on and I need the remote."

"Look, I left the lumps in, just like you like it."

"What lumps? I don't want lumps in my oatmeal. Lumps are for cream of wheat!"

Alice watched Sam search for the remote. "Did you take your medicine dear?"

Sam poked his oatmeal with a spoon. "How do you make lumps in oatmeal anyway? Are these raisins or something?" A bell rings from the kitchen. "Phone" said Sam.

"No, that's the bread I'm baking dear. The lumps are fiber, they're good for you."

Sam reaches into the seat cushion. "It's got to be here somewhere." As he shifts, the television starts up. "See, it went on." A telephone from the show rings. "Alice, the phone is still ringing."

"That's the TV dear, eat your oatmeal."

Sam finds the remote. "Ha, got it. I don't want lumps of fiber, I want lumps of cream of wheat." The doorbell rings. "Alice, please get the phone!"

Alice walks to the door. "That's the doorbell dear. Eat your oatmeal. The doctor said it's good for you. Oh, hi Cathy. What brings you here?"

Cathy peeks in at Sam. "Hi Sam. I just wanted to tell you guys, the movie tonight is supposed to be 'R' rated!"

Alice giggles. "R, how about that? OK, see you there. Sam did you hear that?"

Sam strains to get out of his chair. "I have to go to the bathroom."

The Laundry Room: Ralph was doing the laundry for his wife. He put her clothes and detergent in the washer, turned the temperature dial to hot and waited. When they were done, he put them in the dryer and sat reading the sports page. *Bzzz.* Clothes were dry. "I told her I could do laundry." He folded the red dress and pink underwear, put it in the cart and headed back to the apartment.

The Dining Room: A conspiracy theory was going around that the serving lady didn't like short people. One of the smaller residents compared her meal to the others. "See, your fish is twice as big as mine. And you have more vegetables too."

Her dining companions looked at her sympathetically. A man replied, "I have the chicken with rice."

The Elevator: Margaret pulled her vacuum cleaner while carrying her laundry basket. She walked into the elevator and pressed one for the laundry room. Unfortunately, the cord for the vacuum cleaner had come undone as she walked. A few seconds later Margaret heard a whipping sound, the cord catching between the elevator and the floor she had left. The vacuum cleaner started to bounce up and down from the tension. She took refuge in the corner until the elevator stopped.

Juan, a San Francisco policeman, found the bugs when visiting his mom; the prints came back to Lisa, so he got a techie to reverse the signal on the camera and audio bug, along with a transmitter and placed it in Nana's apartment. The wireless signal was then sent to a police surveillance website.

The tenants were gathering to watch the movie. "Who is this, Clara?"

"Oh, this is my grandson Jeffrey," said Clara.

"What do you do dear?"

Jeffrey said, "I'm an attorney."

After he walked away, Clara whispered. "It's sad, he thinks he's a lawyer, but he just got released from the psych unit at Stanford."

With Nana upstairs at the movie, Lisa arranged to meet Mike at her apartment to look at some of the videos. Lisa pulled up the website and selected her favorite. "This is great, I still can't believe that vacuum cleaner clip," she said laughing. The laughter turned to passion and Mike grabbed Lisa and pulled her to him. Lisa yielded eagerly and within minutes their clothes were off and they were on the living room floor.

But somehow the router in the building picked up the video signal. In the community room where the residents had gathered to watch the movie, Mike and Lisa were now on the big screen. Suddenly, dozens of elderly citizens were being treated to an X-rated show, with Mike the maintenance guy in a leading role!

"This is 'R' rated," said Ralph. "What's the name of this movie? I want to get the DVD."

One of the dining room staff even walked around with refreshments. "Would you like some lemonade?"

An elderly woman reached over and said, "Do you have any popcorn?"

The cook said, "In a minute, we're preheating the microwave."

The Duke of Yelp

"Who is this person?" Said Armen, the owner of the new bakery. Armen looked around at his customers, sitting at café tables, drinking tea or coffee and eating desserts. Meanwhile, John was on his computer in the second floor apartment next door. He was playing a game of hide and seek with Armen.

"Guess it's time to make another appearance" said John. Whenever the café was busy, John came in, bought a cookie, hung out a while and checked in, but since he also checked in from his apartment, Armen had no idea whom the Duke of Yelp was.

The modern coffee house was not a bohemian or flower child flophouse. Instead of a bearded man playing a guitar, there was jazz and spa music coming out of ceiling speakers. Tie-dye cloth and beanbag chairs gave way to expensive leather furnishings expertly matched to create an ambience of warmth and relaxation. At least a dozen people were connected by phone, laptop or iPad, tapping away while talking with companions; heads bobbed and eyes darted up and down. Although Armen was playing catch up, it seemed all young people were skilled in tech use. He just hoped none of them were hacking into his computer to get credit card information.

"Great shortbread," John said to the cashier. "I'll take four."

The dark haired girl with Mediterranean looks selected four unbroken cookies and put them in a bag. "Will that be all?" she said smiling.

"And a coffee," said John as he selected a large take-out cup and lid, then filled it from the self-service decanter. While John was waiting for his change, he tapped on his iPhone, checking in to the location.

Armen heard a ping from his computer and looked around the room. He walked over to his computer, set to the Yelp page that showed his bakery/café. "This one person keeps checking in with the name Pat27. Hmmm. Could be a man or a woman. No picture." He needed another way to find him or her.

A 20-something Asian woman with faded jeans, soft, brown boots and a pink cotton sweater walked in; John's head came to a stop as he saw her. He watched as she bought a tea and raspberry scone, sitting at the corner table and opening her kindle to read. Normally not one to take chances, John decided this was worth the risk. He walked over to her table, paused, presented his bag and said, "Have you tried the shortbread?"

The woman gestured for John to sit down, "No, I would like that. I'm Amy."

John smiled. "John" and he sat down next to her.

"I don't normally take desserts from strangers" she said.

"I don't normally offer them," said John. "Are you from the Mission?" John asked.

"No, the Sunset. My friend is in the wine bar next door."

Armen walked around the seating area, glancing at screens. People continued to come and go. He decided to secretly take snapshots of them with his phone.

John wondered if her friend was male or not; he hoped she would offer this information. "Yes, it looks like a fine place, a little upscale for this neighborhood though."

Amy broke off a nibble of shortbread and swallowed. "Well, that's my friend's way of meeting rich guys."

John put his hand on the table. "And you?"

Amy took a sip of her tea, and then put her hand on the table closer to John. "Money comes and goes. I don't waste it, so I don't need much."

John was feeling comfortable now. "Yeah, me too. But I guess you can tell by the way I dress."

Amy looked John over. "You look fine, do you mean the plaid, flannel shirt?"

John nodded. "Holdover from winters in Berkeley. You?"

Amy leaned forward. "UCLA, but I grew up here. You're not from here, are you?"

How would she know that? John had no discernible accent. "No, Boston. How did you know?" he asked.

"You speak more slowly than natives." After about an hour of social dancing, John and Amy walked out, went up to his apartment and made love.

Back in the bakery, Armen looked at the customer pictures he had on his phone. It was 10:00pm, closing time when a man in a mask came up to the register, pointed a gun at Armen and demanded the money. The gunman tapped something into his phone. "Ping." The dark haired girl took the money out and handed it to the gunman.

You could almost make out a smile from the robber as he turned to leave. "Remember the Duke!"

When the police arrived, Armen showed them John's picture. "This is the guy who's been casing my place."

John escorted Amy back to the wine bar. "Who is this?" said Jenny as she saw John with Amy.

John extended his hand. "John, this is Jenny, a sorority sister visiting from L.A."

Jenny could tell where Amy had been. "So, John what do you do?"

Amy gave her a nudge. "Hands off girl, I saw him first."

John was flattered with the attention of these two beautiful women. "Would you ladies like a drink?"

Amy and Jenny said in unison "champagne please."

In his peripheral vision, John caught them whispering to each other as he walked to the bar. "Three champagnes please, but let's keep it under $25.00."

A waitress from the wine bar pointed out John to a policeman, who was letting them know about the robbery next door. "OK, I see him."

As John and the women were toasting, John pulled out his phone and checked in to the bakery one last time, after they had closed. This would give Armen a laugh when he got in next day; it was just harmless fun.

The policeman, seeing John posting on his phone, confiscated it, looked at the posting for the bakery. "Turn around Pat27, we got you" and led him out the door in handcuffs. "Or should I call you Duke?"

Coq a Doodle Do

Damn French! No wonder they chose this bird as their national symbol. When you think of whining and complaining, who else comes to mind? It all started when Joe moved in with his new wife Barbara. "Joe, please do something about that bird."

Joe grunted and pulled off the covers. "I'm getting my air horn."

Barbara said "No, not that, you'll wake the neighbors."

Joe stumbled to the door. "OK, the hose then."

Joe emailed the local police, explaining the situation. They showed up the next day. "Mr. Mariani, did you send the email about a rooster keeping you up?"

Suddenly Joe felt nervous. "Yes officer, every night there's a rooster waking us up at 3:00 am. I was hoping the town might round him up." The officer took out his pad. "It's been going on each night for a month. Every time a car would drive by, the rooster thinks it's sunlight. And not just car lights. Fire trucks, police cars, ambulances, every lunar phase except a new moon and even lightning sets him off. It started with fireworks on the fourth. That was the longest night ever."

The officer feigned concern. "Tell me where this rooster is exactly?"

Joe gestured him to come in. "Back here" and they walked to the backyard. Then Joe pointed out the vacant county land, over the fence from his bedroom.

"Sorry, sir. You're going to have to contact the county." Needless to say, Joe's attempt at finding the county official in charge of stray roosters was unsuccessful.

Barbara's son Jim stopped by to see if he could catch the rooster. He ran fast, but he couldn't change direction or dive under brush like the bird could. Jim got out his rifle and Pow!

Joe jumped up and ran outside. "Jim, you're gonna get the cops out here."

Jim lowered his rifle. "Sorry Joe, I had a clear shot."

Joe gestured that it was ok. "Did you get him?"

Jim looked back at the bird running. "Almost, they're very fast you know."

That night Joe and Barbara were relaxing in the hot tub on the deck, trying to forget about their confused animal alarm clock. Joe was giving her a back rub. Both of them had their eyes closed. Candlelight around the Jacuzzi set the mood. Then they heard a rustling sound, like squirrels at the bird feeder. When they looked up, the rooster was in the driveway, bobbing his head and walking toward them. Incredulously, the bird walked up the deck stairs and stopped just ten feet from them. Joe looked at the bird. The rooster tilted his head and squeaked. Barbara gaped and whispered. "Throw some hot water on him." Joe scooped up a handful and let it fly. But the rooster was quick and headed back off to his den, like the roadrunner-evading coyote.

Joe had had enough. He went downtown to the animal control office. "Do you pick up stray animals?"

The girl behind the counter replied. "Yes, of course, is it a dog or a cat?"

Joe stammered "a rooster, it's on county property and comes up to our house every night and wakes us up."

The girl frowned. "I'm sorry sir, but roosters aren't covered in our charter. You can rent a trap though."

Joe saw the traps. "All right, then you'll take the bird if I bring it in?"

Another disappointment. "Sorry, we don't take roosters."

Joe took out his money. "OK, give me the trap" and he headed home. He'd worry about what to do with him if he caught him.

Joe lugged the big trap out to the field, put it inside a garbage bag and left a trail of food for ten feet up to and into the trap. How do you catch a French bird? Joe put out French toast and French fries, figuring it would bring literary good luck. That night, Joe and Barbara went to bed hoping to be woken up by something other than 'Coq a Doodle Dos'.

3:00am. This time it wasn't the midnight crowing, but a scream, like a dog had the bird in his mouth. "Barbara, I hope the rooster isn't in a fight." The screaming continued for minutes, then silence. Joe and Barbara gave each other a worried look.

The next morning, Joe walked out to check the trap. Silence. He pulled the garbage bag off the trap. There in beautiful red and brown colors sat the animal. "Oh no, I caught a fox." But when he picked up the trap, the bird came to life and Joe dropped the cage from the surprise. Luckily it didn't open. He practically ran back to the house. "Barbara, I got him." Now what to do with him?

Jim drove up. "Hey Joe, you got him."

Joe interjected. "Yes, but the city won't take him."

Jim had an idea. "I'll take him out to a winery. Should be a safe place for him to crow."

A week of restful sleep did wonders for Joe and Barbara. Now that the rooster was gone, they got back to their normal routines, including intimate dinners and movie nights. Barbara even made French food and rented Casablanca for the evening. Jim stopped by to update them. "Jim, sit, down have some dinner." French hens with country vegetables and wine sauce. Tempting fate, they even had napkins with rooster heads on them. Joe and Barbara were embracing the French now that the bird was gone.

"Delicious mom, but I have some bad news. The bird was doing fine for a while, then one of the vineyard workers found a coyote dragging the carcass away."

Barbara put down her fork and left the table. "Suddenly I'm not very hungry."

Joe looked at Jim. "That news could have waited."

First Love

March 17th, 1978 (New Brunswick, N.J.) - Tony packed his green duffel bag and headed to Newark airport. His dreams of a journalism career on hold, he decided to pursue, for the last time, one Pamela Jean Johnson, formerly of North Augusta, South Carolina. Even though he was leaving college three months before graduation, he was of a singular mindset, to have the love of his life, his first love, the best love he had ever known. Nothing else seemed to matter. It all started eight years ago.

November, 1969 (East Orange, N.J.) – Pam is visiting Laura. Red and orange leaves were blowing around the high school soccer field; the air was a cool 50 degrees. John, Laura's boyfriend, and Tony were moving the ball downfield on attack. When Laura's slow walk passed across John's line of sight, he missed a pass from Tony, turning the ball over.

Tony glanced at John and carped, "How did you miss that?" Then he saw Laura and her cousin Pam, dressed in cotton sweaters, plaid wool skirts, navy blue tights and clogs. They were both 5'9" tall, athletic, with clear, slightly olive skin tones. They each had long, straight hair, cut evenly eight inches below the shoulder; Laura's was dark brown, while Pam's shade was light brown, like stained oak, the same color as her tortoise style, semi-round eyeglasses.

"Never mind" said Tony as he recognized the source of his friend's distraction.

"Who is that with Laura?"

John moved closer so other players couldn't hear his answer. "Her cousin Pam, visiting for Thanksgiving break," said John. Laura and Pam were sharing thoughts that Tony only hoped he was a part of. Pam adjusted her eyeglasses, stroked her hair and whispered something in Laura's ear.

"Double date" Tony said, more like a command than a question, to John as they returned their attention to the game.

On the way off the field after a win, the crowd applauding, Tony and John stopped for a moment to meet the girls. "Pam, this is my friend Tony."

Pam held out her hand. "Hi," her southern accent apparent even in this one syllable.

"Hi," said Tony, the poor kid from Jersey.

John tried to close this favor for his friend. "Laura, maybe Pam and Tony can join us at the movie tonight?"

Laura didn't even confer her cousin replying, "That's just what we were thinking. Pick us up at 7."

As John and Tony left the field for the locker room, Tony turned back for one more look at Pam; framed in the autumn dusk, a long shadow trailing behind, she held Laura's arm and giggled.

Tony slapped John on the back. "John, I'm going to marry that girl."

John laughed. "It's only a first date Romeo. Take some time to get to know her."

Tony and Pam held hands in the theater and whispered to each other, their connection not unnoticed by Laura. "Look" she said to John.

John just smiled. "You'll never guess what Tony said to me earlier" but he didn't tell Laura even as she coaxed him. Later that night getting pizza, the two girls sitting opposite of the boys, you could see that Tony and Pam were becoming closer.

Pam was a proper 17-year-old Christian girl, so anything more than petting was out of the question, even in the era of free love. But Tony was so enamored that he would wait, a long time as it turns out. After spending the week together, Pam returned home. They talked on the phone for the next six months. "Pam, can you come back this summer, stay with Laura?"

At this point, Pam was trying to work this out with her parents. "If I can Tony. My parents want me to work this summer."

Tony had an idea. *Bond's Ice Cream* is looking for help. We could both work there." Both Tony and Pam were going to be seniors, planning for college and the future.

July, 1970 (East Orange, N.J.) – Although Pam was able to come back North, working with Tony didn't happen. Tony worked at *Bonds*, pushing ice cream, while Pam and Laura worked at the new clothing store for teenagers, *The Gap*. Pam had done some modeling for a local store in South Carolina; both she and Laura loved to use their paycheck to buy the latest fashions from San Francisco, the epicenter for this generation. "Oh Pam, you must try this on; it goes perfectly with your eyes."

Laura held the cornflower hippie dress up to her neck. "With crème color knee socks?" said Pam. "Tony will love it!"

Most summer nights, the four had dinner together and listened to music. The Beatles (of course), Three Dog Night, Simon and Garfunkel, Chicago and Rare Earth were putting out new songs while the classics of the 1960s were still popular. MASH and Catch 22 were playing at the movies and poor kids were heading to Vietnam. Richard Nixon was in the White House. The country was splitting up and taking sides.

At the pizza shop, Edwin Starr was pumping out 'War'. "I'm not going to Vietnam," said John. "I'll be in college."

Pam and Laura stopped in mid bite. "John is applying to Rutgers and I'm applying to Douglas," said his girlfriend. Tony knew his family didn't have money for college. "What about you Tony?" said Pam, holding his hand. *'Bridge over Troubled Waters'* started to play.

Tony hadn't thought about this before and didn't know what Pam's plans were. "I'm not sure, maybe RU" looking at her. "What about you Pam?" said John.

Laura nudged her boyfriend, gesturing to be quiet. "Laura wants me to join her at Douglas, but my parents want me to go to a church college closer to home." The jukebox blared *'Give Me Just a Little More Time'*, the plea Tony was thinking about.

It was late August and Pam was going home the next day. Making out in the back seat of Tony's Dodge Dart, on a hill overlooking the skyline of Manhattan, Pam leaned back and asked him the question he had been avoiding. "What about college Tony? Do you think you could go to school in the South?"

Tony knew that out of state tuition, even at a state school, was out of his reach. He would be lucky to get loans to cover Rutgers. "I could do that," he lied "as long as we could be together." Pam smiled and kissed Tony. She seemed satisfied with the possibility for now.

Starting their senior year, Tony and Pam kept in touch in writing or on the phone. It was Tony and John's last year on the soccer team and they enjoyed a championship season. But as John went off with Laura to celebrate after games, Tony could only call Pam, telling her how much he missed her. While time flew by for John and Laura, it seemed like a year until Christmas for Tony. He sent Pam a music box that played Serenade #12 by Mozart. She decided to come up to New Jersey for a week.

January, 1971 (East Orange, N.J.) – It was a week of bliss. Tony and Pam spent most of their time together by themselves, away from their family and friends. Fortunately, college admissions letters hadn't come back yet, saving a discussion Tony dreaded. "I got an early admission to Presbyterian College and I'm still waiting to hear from Douglas" said Pam.

"I'm still waiting to hear from both schools," Tony said. He had applied to Rutgers, but not the private school Pam's parents wanted her to attend.

"So I guess we're still not settled" as she squeezed his hand.

"It will work out," said Tony. She was so beautiful and was wearing the same kind of outfit she had on that afternoon of the soccer game, triggering a love flashback memory. Tony hadn't dated anyone else since they had met, feeling they were destined to be together.

April 14th, 1971. Tony's birthday. Pam had sent him a gift and called him that night. "Happy birthday Tony. I miss you."

Tony had a feeling the college discussion was going to come up. "I miss you too, sweetheart."

A pause. "My parents want me to go to Presbyterian. Did you get in?"

Tony had to modify his lie. "No, sorry," only a half truth" since he never applied. "But there's some bad news. I was drafted, number 28. I'll be heading off to the Army."

Pam began to cry. "No. You'll be sent to Vietnam. What about the college deferment?"

Tony used the political situation to get out of his predicament. "College deferments ended this month. Only a serious medical condition will get you out of the draft."

Pam continued to cry. "I don't want to lose you."

Tony had planned for this. Realizing he didn't have the money for college, he had decided to enlist in the Air Force, avoiding direct combat in Vietnam and giving him money for college. "It's OK, Pam. I'm going to join the Air Force. I won't be going to Vietnam. We can be together after that."

Pam sobbed a little less now. "How long will that be?"

Now Tony choked up a little. "Four years." Tony and Pam spent the next hours remembering the time they spent together and promising to continue their relationship, though it would have to be long-distance.

November, 1971 (Takhli Royal Air Force Base, Thailand) – In the middle of the jungle, Tony was writing his weekly letter.

Dear Pam,

I miss you so much. Even though it's late November, it's very hot, 90s during the day and not much cooler at night. There's no air conditioning, just large fans in the tents we live in. I'm hoping to get stationed at Shaw Air Force Base in Charleston when we leave here. We could see each other again.

All my love,

Tony

Pam and Tony continued to write each other every week, making small talk and expressions of love. After a year in Thailand, Tony was stationed in California, far from his girlfriend. Later, he was sent back to South East Asia, for another year of duty. Toward the end of his third year, the frequency of letters diminished. Then his orders came through, Eglin Air Force Base in the Florida panhandle. It was a nine hour drive to Columbia, S.C. but infinitely closer than he had been since high school graduation. He was eager to write the good news when he opened a letter from her.

Dear Tony,

I am so sorry. It's been so long since we have been together and I have been lonely. I met someone here at college. He's going to be a pastor and he asked me to marry him. I didn't want to say anything before it became serious. I'm going to say yes.

I wish I could have waited for you. I will never forget the time we had together. I hope you find someone as good as you are.

Love,

Pam

Tony knew that Pam had made a difficult decision, one that she wouldn't change. He decided that he would spare them both more pain by not responding to her letter, not writing her anymore or calling her when he returned to the states.

Tony had been taking college courses while he was in the Air Force, to take his mind off the loneliness and to get ahead on his education. Now that he and Pam were finished, he could go to Rutgers on the G.I. Bill and still have money for living expenses.

September, 1975 (New Brunswick, N.J.) – Tony entered Rutgers as a sophomore, having accumulated 36 college credits during his time in the military. John was a senior now and engaged to Laura who went to Douglass, the women's college at Rutgers. Tony and John still hung out together. One day at *Patti's Pizza*, John saw his good friend looking sad. "You still miss her, don't you?" said John.

"Of course I do. She was the best thing that ever happened to me."

John was curious. "Why don't you try to get her back?"

Tony shrugged. "She's engaged. I don't want to ruin that. Even if I wanted to, I'm in school here now and she's graduating."

December, 1977 (New Brunswick, N.J.) - Tony dated many women during college but never found one that made him feel like Pam did. John wanted to cheer him up and invited him to an engagement/Christmas party at Laura's house. Not being attached, Tony decided to go. He arrived with a bottle of wine and an engagement present for the couple. John met him at the door and took the presents. "Hey buddy, thanks. I have a present for you too." Tony looked confused. "Guess who is here?"

Tony's heart began to race. "Pam?" John opened the door and there she was. They rushed to each other and hugged. "What are you doing here? Aren't you supposed to be with your fiancé?"

Pam took his hand quickly to a room away from the guests. Her smile turned to sadness and she began to cry. "We broke up last week. He was cheating on me." She hugged him tightly.

"I'm sorry dear, I'm really sorry," said Tony with genuine empathy. Then he took her head gently, pulled it towards him and kissed her. Pam responded and suddenly they were both reminded how much they meant to each other.

"Laura said I could move in with her this summer, to help her plan the wedding." Tony's world had turned around. This miraculous ending must mean they were meant to be together.

March 10th, 1978. Pam called Tony for their nightly talk. "Tony, my ex has been pursuing me again, begging me to take him back. I don't know what to do." Tony was floored, but tried to remain composed.

"I thought you loved me. I thought we were going to be together again."

Pam began to cry. "I know. I thought so too. I told him I had to think about it and give him an answer at the end of the semester."

Tony didn't want to pressure Pam into her ex fiancée's arms, but need reassurance. "I love you Pam. I will do anything to be with you. It has to be your decision." It was time for a grand gesture, but what?

Spring break had just ended. If he had gone down South during this time, maybe he could have prevented this. But he was busy completing his writing portfolio for graduate school and had a reference from a former professor at Columbia School of Journalism. The next week was torture for Tony and graduate school seemed less important as each day passed.

March 18th, 1978 (Columbia, S.C.) – Tony's plane landed and he rented a car. He found an apartment and put down two month's cash toward the lease. Then he headed to the office of the *Columbia S.C. News*. His writing and photography portfolio in hand, he met with the editor who appreciated this veteran's enthusiasm and gave him a position. Now he had a job and a place to live. It was time to find Pam.

He showed up at her apartment and rang the bell. Pam opened the door. "Tony! What are you doing here?" They kissed. "I was going crazy, waiting to hear from you. I came down and already have an apartment and a job. Pam, will you marry me?"

Pam was in shock. "Tony, I don't know what to say." Tony and Pam made love that night for the first time. Tony knew that it would be magical. Pam thought it would be too, but it wasn't.

She felt so guilty and confused. "Tony, I need more time to think about it." But Tony realized that it wasn't meant to be.

He packed up, returned the rental car and flew back to New Jersey. He finished his senior year but did poorly on his final exams, his heart still broken.

Love, Luck and Fate

Joseph Bosco looked down at the sidewalk, after hearing the bird whistle in the tree overhead. That's when he saw the worn, twenty-dollar bill caught in the stray roots breaking through the sidewalk. "Hmm. How about that?" and he put the bill in his pocket. Joe learned one important lesson growing up. He didn't believe in luck but whenever fortune passed his way, he would say 'it was God's will' and accept it. In fact, Joe attributed everything that happened to him to God's will, good or bad. "Much less stress" he used to say, "much less disappointment too."

Most everyone accepted Joe's philosophy of life. His friends liked the fact that he was so even tempered, never too high or too low. At holiday gatherings, he could be counted on to balance out the histrionics and emotional outbursts of his Sicilian family. At work, he would be the voice of reason when an argument ensued. His matter of fact personality worked just about everywhere, except when he was dating.

***

When Joe was a boy back in 1995, he had his first crush on Sorana Antonelli, a pretty eighth grader in his English class. They were sitting in the movie theater, sharing a box of popcorn. Sorana, like Joe, was from the poor side of town, but that doesn't matter.

"I like your dress Sorana."

"Thanks Joe." Sorana blushed. "I like your shirt."

Joe and Sorana's first date was everything it should have been. Their infatuation continued for two years, until Sorana's parents moved out of state. As it is with young love, both of them were heartbroken. They tried to keep in touch but high school pressures and other interests gradually pulled them apart. Later in life, he wished he had been more persistent and not just accepted their breakup.

***

"Thank Senator." George took the papers from him and filed them into the briefcase. "We have a vote coming up at 2:00pm, so I will pick you up after lunch."

"Get me something at the deli George. I'd like to do some reading. I'll be in my office."

"Corned beef on rye?"

"You know it George."

Senator Joseph Bosco sat in his office reading the paper and eating his lunch when his secretary interrupted him.

"Excuse me senator. You have a visitor."

"Who is it, Hannah?"

"Her name is Sorana Antonelli. She says she's an old friend."

Joe stood up, smiled and gestured her to let Sorana in. He got up to greet her at the door. As Sorana entered, she saw Joe with open arms.

"Senator Bosco, do you remember me?"

"Sorana, you're not allowed to call me senator. How are you?" He gave her a long hug, and then pushed her back while holding on to look at her. "I can't believe it. What's going on with you now?"

"My parents are retired down the shore. The Midwest winters were too much for them now. I came back to visit."

"But they're in good health?"

"Oh, they're fine. Just spending their days walking on the boardwalk and nights watching TV."

"Sit down please. Hannah, get us some snacks and soft drinks please."

"Right away senator. Fruit and vegetable plate and iced tea?" Joe glanced at Sorana for approval, and then gave Hannah the thumbs up. They sat at the round table in the private room adjoining his office.

They each noticed the other's ring finger, naked, providing an answer to one question. "The life of a senator; don't you have anyone special in your life?"

"I was married for a few years, but she died from cancer in 2009."

"I'm so sorry. I shouldn't have asked."

"No Sorana. I'm glad you did. It's time I moved on."

"So you didn't have any children?"

"No, that was a mixed blessing. I wanted a family. What about you?"

"Well, I was engaged for two years, but he cheated on me so we called it off. At least I didn't marry someone who would be unfaithful. But at our age, I'm wondering if I'll ever find love."

"Our age? You're only 31 dear. I'm sure any man would be lucky to have a beautiful and intelligent woman like you."

Sorana blushed. "Well, several have made offers, but after the engagement, I'm hesitant to trust."

Joe took Sorana's hand and looked at her with a gentle smile. "You could always trust me." Sorana put her other hand on top of Joe's, more than just flirting.

"Yes. You were my first and best love."

Hannah noticed the intimate moment and knocked gently on the door. "May I bring this in now?" The senator took his hands away and gestured her in. "Thank you Hannah. That looks perfect." Sorana agreed. Hannah closed the door behind her as she left. Joe and Sorana had an intimate and joyful lunch together.

George knocked on the door. "Senator, it's time for that vote." Joe looked at his watch.

"Thank you George. Is that the only vote this afternoon?"

"Yes senator. You have a rare afternoon off."

"Perfect. Sorana. I have to be away for about an hour, then I'd love to spend the rest of the day with you. Are you free?"

Sorana made a tongue in cheek pretense of propriety. "Yes, senator Bosco. I would like that very much" and shook his hand. Joe rolled his eyes.

"It's Joe, dear, remember? Hannah, would you please help Sorana for the next hour and I'll meet her back here at 3:00."

"Of course senator. Sorana, would you like to go to the Smithsonian for a bit. I can have the senator meet you there."

"Oh, that sounds lovely. Is that OK?"

Joe gave Hannah thumbs up, and then said to Sorana. "Of course, much better. Now you know why I hired Hannah. Have my driver bring her to the museum and I'll meet her there at 3:00."

"Very good senator." Hannah nodded to Joe, then whispered to Sorana. "Sometimes these votes go longer so don't worry if he's a little late."

Joe and George hurried out to make the vote.

Sorana walked leisurely through the museum, admiring the marvels of flight, from da Vinci's flying machine to the space shuttle. She was every bit as lovely as Joe had thought when they were kids, but now she was a striking, mature woman. Her pleated grey skirt over cranberry knee socks, L.L. Bean blouse and cardigan indicated her New England education. She had gone to Boston College, just a few miles from Harvard where Joe went to school. But they never ran into each other there.

Several men made extended glances at her while she walked; Sorana smiled back at them but didn't encourage any more. She was secretly glad that Joe was ready and able for a relationship and she still felt that initial chemistry they had as youngsters.

The senator found her at the museum. He came up behind her and gave her a friendly hug and kiss on the cheek; others noticed this public display of affection. "Isn't that senator Bosco?" said a man who was admiring Sorana.

"I'm afraid so, Bob" said his friend. "Women like that aren't available very long. Looks like the senator has a new love or a mistress."

"Oh, Joe. You made it on time."

Joe took her hand and walked her away from the others. "So, what would you like to do now?"

Sorana squeezed his hand, acknowledging his gesture. "I like the museum but maybe we could go somewhere a little quieter to talk."

As a senator in Washington, D.C., Joe knew all the best places for quiet conversation, whether it was for behind the scenes deal making or for greeting a constituent visiting from New Jersey. They went to one of his favorite cafés and found a table for a glass of wine. They sat in a corner booth, but not completely in private; several people noticed their body language but couldn't hear their conversation. He was not ashamed to be seen in public with a beautiful woman.

"I didn't think I would see you again. Thank you for coming to visit me."

"To be honest, I was hoping it would turn out this way. I have been so blessed except for having someone to share with. That's when I remembered how happy we were as kids. I guess that sounds a little desperate." She lowered her head.

Joe held her hand. "Sorana. You know what I always say. Everything happens for a reason. We were meant to meet again. You are not desperate; you need the right person in your life. So do I. Maybe that's why I haven't moved on."

Sorana felt relaxed and gave Joe a smile that let him know how happy she was. "Is it a problem if we spend time together? I wouldn't want to complicate your public image."

"My image will probably improve being seen with you. My colleagues are always trying to set me up with a lawyer clerking at the court or one of their staff interns. That's not what I'm looking for."

"Well, I'll let you decide how much time you can give me. What hotel would you recommend here?" Her coy question suggested a lot more than a recommendation. Both of them knew where this was going.

"A hotel? Nonsense. You can stay at my townhouse in Georgetown. Where is your baggage?"

"At Union Station in a locker. I took the train from New Jersey."

Joe confirmed his feelings with a hand on Sorana's arm. "That's fine. After our drink, I'll call my driver and we can pick it up. Then we can go freshen up before dinner."

They went to Union Station. Joe went inside while Sorana stayed in the limo. A bird whistled in a tree just outside the entrance. A homeless man sat near the lockers holding a sign that read *can you spare some love?* Joe reached into his pocket and took out the twenty-dollar bill he had found that morning.

"Here you go friend."

The circle was completed. It wasn't luck, just the way it was supposed to be.

The Bridge Game

Hannah and Jim were bridge partners. They knew each other's moves and had an instinct for finessing. No matter what the situation, they were able to adapt and play the right card. Bridge wasn't just a game for them; the deception and gambits were part of their personality. Their best friends, Kate and John, were experienced players, but they didn't have deception in their nature.

Hannah secretly wanted to make John her partner, but not in bridge. She decided she could use Kate to bridge her way to John, if she played her cards right. Not that she didn't care for Jim; she just wanted a little change, if only for a night.

"Would you excuse us gentlemen?" said Hannah. Jim and John rose out of their seats chivalrously while the women went to the ladies room. The two couples had been friends since college, the boys playing on the same soccer team while Hannah and Kate both played field hockey. Athletes make such beautiful mates but sometimes have trouble with commitment.

Hannah examined her makeup in the mirror. "Kate, isn't John's birthday coming up?"

Kate brushed out her chestnut brown hair. "Of course Han, it's this Saturday. "I'm planning a surprise trip to a B&B in Maine."

Hannah feigned interest. "And have you picked out a gift yet?"

Kate looked at her good friend suspiciously. "Why do you want to know?"

Hannah took out her lipstick. "Just curious. Jim's birthday is coming up too. I'm looking for ideas."

Kate relaxed. "Well ok then. I found this lobsterman that will take you out when he gets his traps to choose two choice lobsters. Then when you get back to shore, their restaurant will cook them for you as you sit beside a fireplace listening to jazz, all of John's favorite things."

Hannah held her long, blond hair back and pulled it through red velvet scrunchy. "Well, that will certainly set the mood; did you also get something new to wear?"

Kate winked and held out her phone. "Soma's new chemise, black satin and lace."

Hannah reapplied her lipstick. "Very nice. That should do the trick."

"What about you and Jim? Do you guys have plans?" said Kate.

"I have an idea. You're going up Saturday morning, right?"

"Yes" said Kate, now intrigued.

"Well, I'll get Jim to take me there too. We can have the boys to ourselves all of Saturday, then get together for a surprise Sunday brunch and spend the afternoon together." She gave Kate an encouraging smile.

"OK. That sounds like fun, as long as you don't expect us too early on Sunday." She gave Hannah a knowing wink. "And just make sure you don't run into us on Friday night by accident."

Hannah reassured her. "Don't worry. Just tell me where you're staying and what restaurant you're going to."

Kate was playing right into Hannah's plan.

Jim was well aware of his friend's upcoming birthday. "So John, your 25th is coming up, right?"

John smiled. "Yeah, Kate has some special surprise planned involving a 2-hour drive. I have to wear a blindfold; good thing I have an audible book to listen to."

Jim laughed. "Well, I hope she doesn't kidnap you until you propose."

John smiled at Jim like he had just discovered something.

Jim's mouth opened. "You are going to propose! Good for you my friend. You two are perfect together."

John pulled out the ring. "What do you think?"

Jim pretended to be blinded by the sparkle. "Nice. Will it be a surprise?"

"Yeah. Completely. And since it will be on my birthday, I won't forget the anniversary date."

"Smart, now if you can set the wedding date for a year later, you won't forget any of those dates women want us to remember." Jim and John high-fived. "Just like when we would take the lead with a few minutes left, keep it simple, score, and then play defense."

***

Driving into Freeport, Hannah put her plan into action. "Jim, dear. Here's what I'd like to do today. Let's check in, make love, then do some shopping. Bean's has the new season's clothing in and you need a new jacket."

"OK. And what about tonight?"

"I have a surprise for you. The Celtics are playing the Bulls. You go have bar food and watch the game and then come back to the room at 9pm for dessert." She gave Jim that wink.

"And what are you getting for dessert?" said Jim.

"There's a gourmet cupcake store next to a Victoria's Secret. I'll find something you like."

Chocolate cupcakes and Hannah were two of Jim's favorite meals. "Maybe I should skip the game?"

Hannah shook her head and reminded Jim of post game celebrations in college. "No, you were always hungrier after soccer games" and she leaned over to kiss his neck. "Besides, I want to have an elegant lobster dinner by myself after shopping, not burgers and beer."

Meanwhile, Kate and John dropped off their bags at the B&B, and then joined the captain on his boat to get the lobsters. The salty air and romantic scenery might be the place for John to propose, but he thought he should wait until dinner. He wouldn't want some bounce from a wave to send the ring into the Atlantic. They returned to the restaurant and were seated for dinner, next to a fireplace with jazz music playing, just as Kate had planned.

Kate and John had an intimate dinner, taking their time. John was waiting for the right moment to propose. "During dessert would be perfect" he thought. But when Kate finished her lobster, she got up and motioned John to stay seated.

"Sweetheart, we're going to have dessert and your birthday present upstairs, ok? I'll text you when I'm ready. Relax and enjoy the fireplace."

Kate walked out of the restaurant to their B&B across the street. When she reached the entrance, she saw Hannah. "Han! You're not staying here too, are you?"

"No, Kate. I was just going to meet Jim for dinner. He's watching the Celts at the bar over there" pointing down the street. "Do you have time for a drink?"

Kate looked her watch. "Sure, a quick one. John is still in the restaurant but I told him that I would let him know when to come up. Come, I want to show you this beautiful room we have on the second floor." They quickly walked up the stairway to the corner room overlooking the marina.

"Han, pour us a glass of wine, while I get ready." Hannah nodded as Kate went into the bathroom.

Hannah poured out two glasses, then added a hypnotic to Kate's glass. Hannah knew that the drug would only make her fall asleep for an hour or so, without any memory of what happened.

Kate returned with the sexy new lingerie on. "What do you think?"

"Wow, he's going to be taking that off you really fast. Hope he doesn't tear it." Kate smiled at her best friend's suggestion. Hannah toasted Kate with the wine. "Here's to a great night for both of us. Then we'll see you again for brunch tomorrow at 11."

As they talked, Kate began to sway, and then fell over on the bed. Hannah tucked her in, took Kate's cell phone and texted John.

Your present is waiting in room 3B; get the key and hurry.

Hannah made sure to clear the history of texts from Kate's phone after it was sent. Then she rushed over to her room and got ready for John.

John read the text, left his after dinner drink half-finished, a hundred dollar bill on the check and hurried to the innkeeper. "Room 3B please?"

The man smiled at John, gave him the key and sighed. "Bostonians."

When he got to the door, he found a darkened room, with soft, flickering light from candles and moonlight from the window. Jazz music was playing from a phone on the dresser. The air had a slight scent of Kate's perfume. He undressed quietly, got under the covers, then unknowingly began making love to Hannah; his caresses were received with soft moaning.

"Mmm, John. Don't stop." When John reached her face and kissed her, he realized that this wasn't Kate at all. Hannah smiled sweetly and whispered "happy birthday, sweetie."

"Hannah?" Thinking that Kate must have set this up as his present, John enthusiastically continued making love with the blond schemer.

Meanwhile Kate was sleeping in her room.

After an hour, John was tired but wondering what was next. "Ready to go again?" he asked her.

"Sorry handsome. Time for you to go." Hannah stroked his face. "Wish you could stay. Maybe we can do this again sometime."

John gave her one more kiss, realizing this might be the last woman he would sleep with before getting married to Kate. "Thanks Hannah. You know I've been wanting to do that since college."

Hannah gave him a goodbye hug. "Me too lover. Now back to your room, 2D. Kate's waiting for you."

John found Kate asleep under the covers. He undressed and cuddled up next to her. He began stroking her hair when Kate regained consciousness.

"John, hi. Guess I fell asleep. Happy birthday sweetheart."

"You shouldn't have Kate. This was the best birthday ever and I want to make it even better." He took the ring out. "You are the one I want to spend my life with. Please marry me."

Kate perked up. "Yes, of course I will." Then the newly engaged couple made love and slept until morning. Kate never remembered seeing Hannah or being drugged.

Back in room 3D, Hannah had to clean up before Jim returned from the bar. She arranged the cupcakes along with champagne on a table. She took a quick shower, brushed her teeth and hair, and then changed into the new lingerie from VS. She was careful not to leave any clues of her deception. Then she heard a knock on the door, noticed that it was 9 o'clock and answered sweetly. "Come in."

Jim came in and quickly undressed. "Perfect."

"Would you like some champagne and cupcakes, sweetheart?"

"Those can wait, I'm ready for dessert first." Jim and Hannah were very good together and Jim never realized what had happened earlier that night. They made love, had champagne and cupcakes and then made love once more. Then they both slept in.

Hannah got up first, showered, dressed, then woke up Jim. "I found a great place for brunch. We have a reservation for 11. You get ready. I'm going out to get some last minute things at Beans."

Jim gave Hannah a hug and kiss. "OK, dear. I'll wait for you downstairs at 10:45."

Hannah left the B&B quietly, before John and Kate would be leaving for brunch. She got in her car and headed for L.L. Bean, about a mile away. As she drove, she remembered her night with John, how she finally got to make love with him and wondered how life would have been different if she had been with him. One night was not enough for her; she was considering a longer affair, something she would have to keep from Kate. She decided to send John a text. But it would have to be innocent enough to keep Kate from getting suspicious.

Happy Birthday John! I hope I can find something special for you when you get back to Boston.

After hitting 'send', she looked up and realized her car was heading straight for a canal, as the winding roads in Maine will do. She turned the wheel just in time to avoid the water, but hit the bridge hard. The air bag deployed and she lay there unconscious.

231

The Lighthouse

(Seal Cove, CA – 1969) The air was moist and salty. The sky was blue with cumulus clouds floating slowly from West to East. A lighthouse peered out towards the Pacific Ocean waiting for her nightly shift. Tim lived within walking distance in a small, pale grey Cape Cod home with red shutters. He was the light keeper and resident artist in the sleepy town of Seal Cove.

The lighthouse had a wide bottom with enough room for hostel travelers going to San Francisco. There was a stained, oak plaque, engraved with the name 'Wentworth' in the center of the door. A cowbell with a rope cord was affixed to the left, Tim's doorbell.

A boy and a girl, dressed in baggy clothes, walked up to the cottage and pulled the heavy rope back and forth to ring the bell. "Hello. Is anyone home?"

Tim answered. "Yes, hello. Are you looking for the hostel?"

The girl spoke first. "How much is it for the night?"

"Eight dollars a person each night and that includes breakfast." Tim could tell that even eight dollars might be a lot. "But tonight it's eight dollars for a couple."

The two smiled and reached into their jeans to find the money. The boy pulled out three ones and some change and the girl found a five dollar bill. "Here you go sir" as she handed the wrinkled bills to Tim. "Is there a place to wash up?"

"There's a shower in the house," Tim said pointing behind him. "And there are two bathrooms in the lighthouse. My name is Tim."

"I'm Hannah and this is my boyfriend Eric. We're coming down from Oregon."

"Welcome. Let me show you the lighthouse." The couple followed Tim, holding hands. Tim pulled open the heavy metal door with a creaking sound you would expect, gesturing for them to enter first. The floor was rectangular with a black iron, spiral staircase in the middle. Along the sides were green army cots, at least 10 and more space for people with blankets and sleeping bags. The floor was clean and there were no signs of bugs. "Well, here is where you sleep. On the next landing up, there are two bathrooms and a sink. There's also a small fridge with bottled water."

Eric pointed to the huge windows surrounding them. "There aren't any shades?"

"Sorry" said Tim. "It is a lighthouse" and he gave a little chuckle at his joke.

"Don't worry, folks get pretty tired by dark and sleep soundly. It's the salt air and ocean breeze. Hear that whistling. That's the wind blowing through."

"There's no heat?" said Hannah.

Tim pointed up. "Not regular heat, but when the lamp starts spinning, it radiates heat down here, sort of like sleeping near a campfire. You'll be fine in your bags."

Hannah and Eric put their backpacks and sleeping bags on two of the cots, facing the ocean. "How many people are here tonight?"

"Only two now, but two more have called in to reserve a spot. The two over there are your age, another couple. From Arizona I think. Susan and Jim. Nice kids. They went into town to get something to eat at the diner. You just walk down that street about a half mile and you can't miss it."

233

"Thanks Tim. If it's OK with you, we'll use the shower and then go into town." Eric nodded his agreement.

"Sure enough. Just walk in the back door. There are towels, soap and shampoo. Breakfast is from 7 to 9, bacon, eggs, pancakes and juice. Oh, and coffee and tea of course. You could walk to the diner if you want something more, but you have to pay."

"I'm sure your breakfast will be fine Tim. Besides we want to get an early start; we're trying to make the music festival in Berkeley by Saturday." Eric pointed to his mandolin case and Hannah's flute.

"Well, isn't that wonderful. Maybe you'll play something for me later."

"We will Tim." Tim walked back to the house. Eric and Hannah realized how tired they were and collapsed on the cots. They woke up at four, in time for that shower and walk to town for dinner.

As they were walking into town, they saw another couple. "That must be Susan and Jim." When they met, Hannah introduced herself. "Hi. Are you staying at the lighthouse too?"

Susan spoke first. "Hi, yes, I'm Susan and this is Jim. We've been there for a week."

Jim shook hands with Eric. "Hi, Eric and Hannah."

Eric was wondering why they had been here so long. "Been here a week, huh?"

"Yeah, we just love it here. The fresh air, the beach and that lighthouse." Susan gave Jim an affectionate hug. "We have the wildest dreams in there."

Eric and Hannah looked a little surprised. "Dreams? What do you mean wild?"

Jim and Susan just giggled. "You'll see," and they continued walking back to the lighthouse.

Eric and Hannah found a booth at the diner, ordered dinner, then asked the waitress. "You know anything about the lighthouse?"

The waitress smiled. "This is your first night, kids. Well, I wouldn't want to spoil the surprise" and she walked back to the kitchen.

Eric stopped her. "Wait. Could you bring us some water too?"

The waitress giggled and nodded. "Sure thing hon."

Hannah rubbed her forehead. "Sounds like an adventure. Wonder why Tim didn't say anything."

"Beats me. Maybe the place is haunted."

"Eric. You don't believe in ghosts, do you?"

"I don't know what I believe until I see it. But nobody's said it was scary, just smiled and laughed about it."

"Maybe even sensual" as Hannah slid her foot under Eric's jeans.

"Hmm."

***

When Eric and Hannah arrived back at the lighthouse, they saw Jim and Susan sitting outside behind the railing, watching the sun set over the ocean. "Hey guys. You seem to have found the perfect place."

"This is like heaven. If you watch carefully, you can see seals out in the cove chasing dinner. There's one now" said Susan as she pointed it out.

"Oh yeah. Cool. Mind if we join you?"

"Not at all. Would you like some wine?"

"Great, thanks."

Susan poured some sangria into plastic cups and handed them to Eric.

"Thanks Susan. Hey, let me get my music."

"Bring my flute honey."

"OK, be right back."

"A concert on the ocean?"

"No, just a little music to go with the view. Eric and I are renaissance musicians. We're supposed to play at the Berkeley festival on Saturday."

"Right on. Hope you get there in time."

"We have four days. We should be able to hitch there by then."

"Oh, getting a ride isn't the problem. We thought we would leave after one night."

Hannah gave Susan a quizzical look. "The wild dreams?"

"The wildest girl, the wildest."

Eric returned with the mandolin and handed the flute to Hannah. "OK, any requests from the sixteen hundreds?" and he laughed.

"Fraid not. Just do your thing."

Hannah began with the flute and Eric joined in. It was a lyrical song, just as you would imagine from 17th century England. "I can almost smell the roasting pig now" Jim said.

"Don't forget the jousting and bow and arrow competitions" said Eric.

"And ladies in corsets tied up to their breasts" said Susan, smiling at them.

"M'lady, I think they are flirting with us," said Eric.

"I think you're right, kind sir," said Hannah.

The four of them talked and played and danced, finishing two bottles of wine. The sun was almost set now and it was getting dark. They could see Tim approaching with a flashlight.

"Time to light the lamp," he said.

Jim and Susan stood and applauded. Eric and Hannah just looked on, perplexed. Tim walked up the spiral staircase and turned on the lamp. Then he set the motor for rotation. A loud whirring sound turned into a low hum as a bright beacon lit up around them.

"OK, time for bed," said Jim.

"But it's only 8:30?" said Hannah.

"You'll see." Jim took Susan's hand and they ran inside giggling.

Tim saw the other couple. "Better get inside. The wind will kick up and blow you right onto those rocks down there. Remember, there's water in the cooler on the second level."

When they got in, they saw Jim and Susan already making out in their sleeping bags, with their clothing tossed out on the wooden floor. Susan started to make sounds of excitement, unabashedly in front of them.

Hannah put her hand to the floor. "Oh, I see why they haven't left. The floor vibrates from the lamp turning."

"Sounds good to me" and he took his clothes off and jumped into the sleeping bag.

Susan saw Eric. "Wait, you don't have your water" as she pointed up the staircase.

"Water. I'm not thirsty."

"You will be hon. Trust me."

"I'll get it Eric." Hannah scurried up the staircase and returned with two bottles of water. By this time, Susan was in her second round of ecstasy.

Hannah gave a bottle to Eric, they clicked the plastic as if they were glass bottles, and then they took a long gulp. "Cheers." She got into the sleeping bag and took off her clothing.

"Hannah. Is the room spinning?"

"No, Eric. That's the lamp spinning above us. It's making a shadow spin around the room. Wait. I feel it now too."

Susan and Jim continued their lovemaking, the empty bottles of water lying beside them. Eric noticed this and said to Hannah. "Have more water." They both finished their bottle, and then realized what was happening.

"It's the water," said Hannah. "I can feel the spinning now and some..ooh..oh..."

"Come here Hannah," said Eric and they too lost their inhibitions, now oblivious to Susan and Jim. After a couple hours, all four of them fell asleep. That's when the dreams started.

Susan dreamed of flying on the light beam from the lighthouse toward the moon. She laughed and danced among the clouds.

Jim saw animals in a multi-colored jungle. He stalked around like a leopard, chasing his prey. Then he became the leopard and ate a rabbit.

Eric was back in the 1600s, jousting against an evil giant. Riding at full gallop, he thrust his lance into the giant, who fell to the ground with a large thud.

Hannah, well Hannah had the most exquisite dream of all. She was a princess at a ball, dancing with a handsome man, not a prince, but a commoner. No one else seemed surprised by this and Hannah fell back as her companion dipped her to kiss. Then he picked Hannah up and carried her off.

But all the dreams were interrupted by a loud noise, the heavy door banging. Then they saw a light coming in at their eyes, blinding them. "Who's there?" said Eric.

"Sorry to wake everyone. It's just Tim with some latecomers. Everyone, this is Rachel and Dan."

Everyone exchanged obligatory pleasantries in spite of being woken up out of their dreams of ecstasy.

As Tim turned to leave, Hannah called out. "More water please."

Respectable Sinners

Peter came out of the gas station store with two bottles of Hawaiian water, handing one to Maria as she filled her tank. "You're an angel, showing me heaven today" he said, stroking her hair slowly and whispering into her ear.

Maria smiled, nuzzled under his neck and held Peter's hand. "You're too good to me Peter. When will I see you again?"

"Soon sweetheart. You know I can't live without you. I'm on a business trip this Wednesday. You can meet me in Carmel. I have a suite on the ocean for three days. I'll make sure you have the days off."

Maria closed her eyes and sighed. "I can't wait. I should get back now, laundry to do." She kissed him and finished filling her Honda Civic. Peter got into his Land Rover. They talked on their cell phones as they pulled out, smiling furtively.

Bob couldn't hear what they were saying, but it was clear that Peter, married and Maria, who wasn't, were having an affair. Peter was in his late fifties; Maria couldn't be more than twenty-two. Also, Maria was Peter's housekeeper. This was a rare glimpse into the private lives of Bob's congregation, although he suspected this was a common situation. He headed back to the church.

Bob's flock wore tailored clothing, drove luxury cars and ate fine food. They sent their children to the best schools. They took politically correct positions on the issues and voted for whatever candidate would maintain the status quo. They give to charity, volunteered occasionally and attended fund-raising dinners for socially approved causes. They had so many diversions to fill their lives that they hardly ever had time to think of the big picture.

It was one of those small, exclusive towns where only the fortunate few lived, where old money and new money lived comfortably side by side in homes with ocean views, nannies and housekeepers. A sophisticated system of surveillance cameras and a vigilant police force kept the residents safe; safe enough where children could play outside and walk to school alone.

But this was no Peyton Place; adults kept their affairs discreet and gossip was unheard of; in fact, talking about indiscretions would make you an outcast. Everyone was very happy to maintain a facade of respectability, not only for the children but also for their own peace of mind. After all, sin is only sin if it's out in the open and there is always time to repent before your life is finished.

So Bob had difficulty discovering the sins of his flock. The members gave generously for services rendered, mission requests and other charitable causes he brought to their attention. No, there wasn't any dysfunction at First Presbyterian, just a utopian community of privilege. He entered his office to see his junior pastor, Scott, preparing for a youth sermon.

"Scott, tell me something. How are the kids doing?"

"Fine pastor. I've never seen a better-adjusted group of kids. They seem to live an idyllic life without stress. Why do you ask?"

"I've been wandering around town the last few weeks and I've noticed some more disturbing behavior. Corruption, deceit and adultery topping the list, all from our congregation."

"Another affair. Hmmm. That's seven this week. Who may I ask is it this time?"

"Peter Robinson and his housekeeper Maria. I saw them at the Shell station. They didn't notice me, but anyone could have seen them and they didn't seem to care."

"Well, Peter's wife Joan is sleeping with the tennis pro at the club, often *at* the club!"

"You have confirmation of this?"

"Yes sir. The cameras are working perfectly. It's all in our database." Scott had managed to intercept the town's security cameras, as well as place his own mini cameras in more private spaces indoors.

"Scott, this is the first church I've seen where sin is so rampant and yet discreetly hidden from others. Maybe that's why the children seem so healthy. Usually, you'll find the men at the club bragging about their conquests and women chatting about it in the spa or cafés, but not here."

"I'm going out tonight to install more cameras. Four more restaurants, the new yoga center and the street artists."

"Those musicians, jugglers and magicians in the town square? What do you hope to catch there?"

"I've seen some unusually large tips landing in the hats lately, along with notes folded around them and flirting, especially between the women and the magician and a disturbing flirtation between a cougar and a guitar player. And the time when they take their breaks is corresponding to these tips. Something is going on all right."

"And how many of these people have we confirmed now, Scott?"

"One hundred and ninety three pastor, all from our congregation."

"None from the synagogue?"

"No sir, not one. It's all on us."

"Well, it's a good thing Rabbi Goldman doesn't know about it. He would give me hell."

"Yes sir."

"Which brings us back to our problem. We have a congregation full of deceitful, deceptive sinners, all quietly leading very comfortable lives, making millions of dollars, both legally and illegally and sleeping with each other. But no blow-ups, no filing for divorce, no drama at all. How is this possible?"

"It's a New Age Sodom and Gomorrah, pastor. And we're responsible for cleaning it up. But I've been thinking and may have an answer."

"Anything Scott, let's hear it."

"Well, preaching to them isn't working. They don't consider sin a problem. They think life is what you make it and the afterlife is an after thought, or no thought at all."

"Right."

"I've created aliases, anonymous characters with an untraceable email address. I call them Tom or Nancy, depending on whom I'm addressing. They send an email each day to someone in our congregation detailing their sins and hints that they are compiling evidence to deliver to the wronged individual or business. But not a threat so much as an opportunity to repent."

"Yikes. A bit radical, don't you think?"

"As long as we maintain our ignorance of what's happening, I think we'll be all right. We've tried to gently nudge them in the right direction on Sundays, but the sermons seem to be providing more ideas for sinning than for correcting the sinners."

"OK Scott. Go ahead and start the emails, but don't mass email yet, just ten a day."

"Any particular sin we should start with? We seem to have an overlap between adulterers and business people, especially women."

"All right. Start with those people who are committing multiple sins. Put Peter Robinson and his wife Joan on top of the list. They have three children."

"Right. That family is a disaster waiting to happen."

"And keep me updated on those street artists. That's too conspicuous."

"Is there any difference between public and private sins pastor?"

"Good question. Public sins can influence others more directly, but I think private sins are more insidious because the sinners think that there are no consequences."

Scott broke into the new yoga center that night, the first time his military background was put to use after seminary. He placed mini cameras in the locker rooms and in the main workout center, cleverly inserted into the fragrant fresh plants that were already in place. From there he headed to the town square to rig up some trees focusing on the area where the street artists performed. Finally at 3:00am, he broke into four restaurants and again placed mini cameras in plants facing quiet corner booths.

Scott's scheme went into effect the next day. Emails were sent out to the first group, detailing, with video clips, the transgressions he had recorded earlier. He even sent an email to a local politician whose campaign was corrupted by the opposition. Then he tracked the recipients to see if their behavior changed.

A lunch business meeting between a banker and a financial advisor at one of those restaurants provided immediate results. Although neither wanted to admit to seeing compromising video of their corruption, both knew they had to adjust their methods.

"John. The reason I thought we should hold meetings here is that I'm concerned about electronic bugging at the office. This looks more like a casual lunch instead of the culmination of our Machiavellian plan to bilk investors."

"That makes sense Bill. No paper or electronic trail, just friendly talk among financial professionals. We could even say we were planning a community fundraiser for the poor."

Bill replied with a sly smile. "You mean those making less than one million dollars a year?"

John twirled the swizzle stick in his glass of Scotch. "Yes, those poor bastards. Now where is lunch? Ah, here it comes, my twenty-four-inch porterhouse, onion rings, avocado and Hollandaise sauce."

"John. Didn't your doctor tell you to lose weight?"

John wiped some sauce from his lip. "Hey, I'm having fruits and vegetables here. Besides, you only live once gentlemen. I intend to enjoy it."

A nursery deliveryman rang the doorbell of the Robinson house. Maria answered it. "Yes, what is this?"

"Plants for the home, courtesy of the club."

"Oh, they're lovely. How many are there?"

"Sixteen, one for each room. Mrs. Robinson admired them the other day. I can put them in the rooms for you."

"Thank you. Let's start upstairs and finish here."

Meanwhile, Linda Fleming, who lost the recent election for mayor, was meeting with her staff to figure out how they could go from a ten-point lead in the polls to losing on election day. "Where did our supporters go? Sally Johnson did something to turn our voters. She's just a realtor. She doesn't have any experience in office. How did she do it?"

Her aide looked over a clipboard. "She made some promises to homeowner associations and some deals with the bank for favorable refinancing. She was able to turn a thousand voters at the last minute. We just got proof of it from an anonymous source."

"Well, we're going to strike back. If they can use technology to steal an election, then we can use it to smear her reputation. Get me that intern, Segretti's grandson."

One of the reasons that Fleming lost the election was her pollster. Instead of checking with voters before and after the vote, she was taking a nap in the adjacent building. If she had been doing her job, Fleming would have had some notice before the election was over and may have been able to counter her opponent's strategy in time. Sometimes sin takes the form of inaction.

At the yoga center, the pampered wives took their morning exercise before heading to the cafés. Scott monitored the feed from the mini cameras. One of the women passed a note to the instructor, an Italian fitness model, inside of a small towel; she discreetly opened it up, and then smiled. As she walked about the class, she paused to whisper something to her amante and touched her back. Scott had to review the digital tape in slow motion to catch the proof but the intentions between the pair were clear in any language.

That evening, people strolled the town square window-shopping the boutiques. Husbands and wives held hands while children carried ice cream cones. The salty summer air blew in from the ocean. At the entrance to the park, the street artists were displaying their skills. Jugglers, magicians and musicians performed to the crowds, while a hat for tips filled up with change and bills. Every so often, a note would drop in. A bearded guitar player winked at the fifty-something fit woman leaving her message of an upcoming rendezvous. But Scott caught it all. As the guitar player read the note, Scott's mini camera zoomed in and snapped a picture. He then relayed it to the woman's husband, the principal of the elementary school, who coincidently was at the time doing some professional development with the new second grade teacher who just so happened to be married to the guitar player.

"What a mess" Scott said to himself. "No one would believe this if it was one of those trashy novels the women read on the beach."

The next day Scott checked the cameras he delivered in the houseplants at the Robinson home. He couldn't have hoped, or dreaded, what he discovered.

Peter cornered Maria in the bedroom cleaning up. "I need you now lover."

"Oh!" Maria said. "Peter, we've never done this here."

"Sorry. This can't wait." Peter ripped off Maria's clothing, threw her on the bed and had his way with her for the next hour.

The tennis pro dropped Joan off at her house following their lesson. "Thanks for the ride Jason. Why don't you come in for a cold drink?"

As soon as they were in the kitchen, Joan pulled Jason to her, grinding her hips onto his. Jason was excited but worried. "Joan, we don't do this here."

"We do today Jason." Both couples miraculously finished their lovemaking without running into each other. Jason went back to the club. Peter slipped out the back and went to the office. Joan took off for the spa. That night Peter and Joan had a quiet and friendly dinner with the children.

But Scott had it all on tape. He sent the compromising video clips to Peter, Joan, Maria and Jason.

***

The next day, Pastor Bob got his morning coffee from the pretty barista, and then sat down to read his paper. Rabbi Goldman saw his friend and sat next to him. "Bob, how are things going?"

"You know David. I've discovered that you have to save the congregation one at a time."

"Mazel Bob. Me ken dem yam mit a kendel nit ois'shepen."

"Sorry David, I don't know that one."

"The ocean cannot be emptied with a can."

"From your mouth to God's ears David."

The Rich are Going to Hell

"Why would he say that?" The gentrified couple couldn't believe what they were hearing.

"It's just to get our attention," whispered the woman to her husband. "It must be about being thankful for what you have."

The husband adjusted his glasses. "I don't see the point. We don't have to put up with this" and they left brusquely. The preacher continued without hesitating.

The audience was adorned with khaki slacks, polo shirts and topsiders. The tax lawyer in the third row queried his second (trophy) wife. "We take time out on a Sunday to come here and this is what we hear."

The preppy blonde with the degree in art history agreed. "This is in very poor taste. We could have gone to the beach." Their attention was drawn back to the speaker.

"Look at your cars, your homes, your vacation homes and your country clubs. Do you think they make you a better person? Do you think you have some special blessing from above? No, you're the same as the homeless man in the street, the poor woman who takes the bus to clean your house, the laid off teacher struggling to feed her children."

Old money and nouveau riche sat side by side this morning. There was a tailored man in a seersucker jacket, crisp Brooks Brothers oxford and pastel blue tie who looked like he just landed from Martha's Vineyard. Next to him was a woman in pinstripe blue and power tie, obviously a Wall Street broker. She leaned over to her friend and spoke. "I thought this was going to be about the goodness of money, how it's a sign of being blessed."

"Look at your life. What do you think about? What do you do each day? How much time do you give to self-examination, peeling back the layers and finding out what your core really is? Who among you can say 'I have earned everything I have?'"

People started to file out, first one by one, then in small groups. The congregation of about 100 quickly dwindled to just a couple dozen willing to listen.

"But not everyone wants to hear" he said gesturing to the people exiting the tent. "They don't want to give up their comfortable life or face the fact that their life has been wasted in the pursuit of money. Who here is willing to peel away the layers of shame in public, to examine their life in full view of God and this audience?"

A man in his thirties timidly raised his hand. "Thank you son. Don't be afraid. Come up here and tell us your story."

The man took the microphone. "My name is Alex. I made a lot of money with an Internet scam that preyed on the elderly. I'm ashamed of what I have done."

The preacher nodded as he placed his hand on the man's shoulder. "We have all sinned son. Repentance starts with confession. What do you want to do now?"

Alex cleared his throat and continued. "I could send a gift anonymously to all those I cheated."

The man of the cloth looked up. "Anonymously? Will that clear your conscience Alex?"

Alex responded, "What else can I do?"

The preacher replied, "Get down on your knees and pray, in front of your brothers and sisters, so that you may be cleansed."

The man knelt down as the preacher held the microphone for him. "Now admit what you have done son."

Alex spoke into the mike. "I have stolen money and ruined the lives of decent honest people. I have done this without guilt or remorse."

The preacher reassured Alex. "This is the start of a new life. Through your confession, you can begin again. Go and sin no more."

Suddenly, two men hustled the speaker off his pulpit, dragging him away from the congregation. This surprising incident shocked the listeners, many of who whispered to their companions with explanations of what just happened. Everyone finally left the tent toward the row of BMWs and other luxury cars. On their way out, the trophy wife asked her husband. "Why do you think this guy was speaking at a car dealership anyway?"

The Tightrope

In America today, there are many towns adjacent to each other with extreme differences in culture, wealth and education. There is a specific dividing line between these towns, but you don't need any signs to tell when you have crossed over. It makes you wonder if one town is blessed and the other one is cursed. Or maybe both towns are cursed.

Some people, like Juan, lived in both worlds. Each morning, he drives his pick up truck into town, past manicured lawns and fruit trees, to a construction site downtown. Oak Park's town council decided to makeover Main Street with gas lamps, cobblestones, benches and topiary, resembling something out of 19th century England. While he was working, Juan was accepted here, although not seen. Once the Sun went down, when those fortunate few were assembling for dinner, he lit up like one of those new gas lamps.

Justin, one of the fortunate few, walked into the French restaurant with his girlfriend, Karen, the kind of girl you want to be seen with. Karen had the right looks, the right education and the right family. She dressed classically, sporting a blue skirt, white ruffled top and camel hair blazer. Her hair was straight, shoulder length and blonde, which only brought attention to her blue eyes and perfect skin. She worked as a junior associate in a local law firm, the same one where Justin was applying. Justin wasn't dating Karen to help get the job, but it wouldn't hurt, so long as he was discreet about it. Justin and Karen had one thing in common, a comfortable life, neither having had experienced the struggles that people like Juan had overcome.

Juan put his tools into the lock box of his truck and headed home. It was only three miles away but East Oak Park seemed more like one of those cities you see on the news, where some gang banger killed an innocent child. Driving past graffiti-filled walls, a 24-hour convenience store and a run down elementary school, Juan was quickly reminded of his world, one where the night brought out drug dealers, prostitutes and the people addicted to them. In Oak Park, strollers would be listening to the chamber music softly playing from the rock gardens he had helped create; here, anyone walking would hear the loud and vulgar sounds of boom boxes and cars with heavy bass accents, cruising slowly while their passengers watched for prey. Turning the corner, he saw his church. "Maybe I should stop in and say a prayer," he thought. But he was hungry and decided to go home.

Justin examined Karen while she read the menu. What did she see in him? Karen could have anyone she wanted. It wouldn't surprise him if someone at the firm were propositioning her. Maybe one of the senior partners, ready to exchange their first wife for a trophy or one of the rich clients she saw daily.

"I'll have the Waldorf salad, Salmon with truffles and Pommes de Terre au gratin" she said in fluent French.

"Shrimp salad and the steak Bordelaise, medium" said Justin, trying to keep up.

Juan's wife Ines was putting dinner on the table; rice, beans, cheese and vegetables melted in a casserole dish. He could hear his seven-year old son Manny and ten-year old daughter Dania playing in the other room.

"Dania, take Manny to wash hands and come to dinner...Daddy's home." Juan hung up his jacket and kissed Ines on the cheek. "How was your day?" he said. Ines worked part-time in the school cafeteria, serving free breakfasts to kids who wouldn't get anything at home.

"That school," she sighed. "Even the young ones are acting like punks now, flashing gang signs and wearing their pants down to here" as she gestured to her upper thigh. "At lunch, some fifth grader made a gun sign with his hand when I told him he couldn't have seconds."

Juan shook his head and thought about the kids in Oak Park, dropped off from their parent's BMW's, Mercedes' and SUV's. "Two public schools but you would never know it," he thought. "But no trouble for Manny and Dania?"

"No, they're fine, I keep an eye out for them."

The waiter brought a shrimp salad to Justin and the Waldorf to Karen. They sipped their wine, ignoring the waiter. "So, how's the real world of law?" Justin asked.

Karen responded without looking up from her salad. "We had a deposition today for a man accused of embezzling from his family business. It's pretty clear that he did it."

Justin indicated that he was listening. "Oh, so what's your strategy?"

Karen smiled. "We'll get him off. His father was sleeping with the secretary and will settle once we show him the pictures." Karen looked up and touched Justin's hand. "Did you hear from the bar yet?" Justin had failed the bar exam the first time he took it.

Dating him was Karen's way of slumming it. "Should be online any day now; I'm pretty sure I nailed it this time."

Karen winked. "Did you check it today?" knowing that the results had been posted. "Go ahead, check."

Justin pulled out his phone, entered the web address and signed in. "Hey! I passed," showing the screen to Karen. He leaned over and kissed her.

Karen replied, "Good, I had planned a little celebration for tonight."

Ines, Dania and Manny bowed their heads while Juan said grace. "Lord, thank you for this meal and for our children. Please care for us and for those less fortunate that do not have food tonight. We pray this in your name. Amen."

Ines filled the children's plates first. "Is there another job after you finish this one?" she asked.

Juan nodded his head as he ate some vegetables. "I think so. My boss said Oak Park wants to extend the project to the town hall and courthouse. That should take another six months at least." This news came as a relief to Ines who was worried about Christmas presents and utility bills. Ines paid the bills each month, taking some stress off of Juan. He didn't realize how some past due notices had come because Ines was very good at juggling their paychecks and credit.

"God bless those poor people! What would they do without cobblestone streets and gas lamps?" said Ines.

"Don't forget the benches and Japanese gardens with the music playing" said Juan.

"Well, their good fortune means work for you Juan, don't forget that."

Juan smiled and agreed. "Yes, where would I be without the fortunate few?"

Justin was looking down at his steak. "Look at this. I said medium and this is medium well."

Karen looked up from her salmon and examined his steak. "Yes, you're right. You should send it back." She gestured to the waiter and gave him instructions. "I want tonight to be special for you!"

Justin wondered what other surprises Karen had for him. "Won't we be late for...." when Karen interrupted.

"For what? You don't know what I have planned?" Justin rolled his wine around the glass and caught Karen's expression. "You'll see," and this time her expression confirmed the fantasy he had already started. Justin tried to contain his enthusiasm, tried to play it cool. He was dating up here and both of them knew it.

The children were watching some game show on television while Juan helped Ines clean up. He pulled a small box from his pocket. "I bought you this," and handed it to her. Her first thought was the money. His first thought was making her happy.

"Juan, I've told you not to buy me things. Save money for the children." Juan watched Ines' expression as she opened the box and saw the charm bracelet. Ines drew her breath in and hugged Juan. "Thank you dear, it's so beautiful." Two of the charms had the names of their children and one the name of Ines' mom who had passed away in the summer. When she saw that, Ines started to cry.

"Now, now, no crying" as he took out his handkerchief and wiped off the tears. "This should be a celebration!"

This time Justin's steak was cooked perfectly. He ate quickly enough to finish without Karen noticing. "So, can you give me a hint?" hoping to encourage her to end the suspense.

"OK, but it's not here" her voice and head gesturing that it was close.

"So it's in town?" he said as he took the last sip from his wine glass.

Karen was enjoying the torture now. "Finish your steak dear" while she patted her mouth with her napkin. "We have a few more minutes before it will be ready."

Juan put the leftovers in the refrigerator and thought about lunch tomorrow. There was cold chicken he could slice up for a sandwich, some cheese, an apple and some cereal. Juan liked to snack on cereal on his breaks. It was better than junk food.

"I'll drive" said Karen and motioned Justin to the passenger side of her BMW. Justin's imagination was flickering like one of those jump cut commercials that only show you a split second of a hundred scenes. When Karen said, "close your eyes and lean toward me," he expected a tender kiss. But Karen put one of those dark sleeping masks on him; the kind people wear to keep out the light. "OK, sit back, we'll be there soon," and she laughed a little.

At this point, the scenes in Justin's commercial had taken another turn and he could feel his pulse quicken. It might be the adrenalin flowing when he said, "should I be scared?" still trying to play it cool.

"You should be if you take off that mask, mister." But taking off the mask was the last thing Justin was going to do. He was enjoying this too much and wasn't going to blow his surprise.

"Bedtime Manny, bedtime Dania. Go brush your teeth now" Ines said in her firm but loving mom voice. The kids scurried obediently. After they finished the dishes, they could hear mumbling from the bedroom.

"I'll tuck them in, you sit and relax" said Juan. Manny and Dania were under the covers in the small room they shared, just big enough for a bunk bed, toys and stuffed animals. "Did you say your prayers?"

258

"Yes Daddy" they said, almost in unison. "We prayed for you and mommy too."

Juan realized what a blessing his children were, not like those punks at their school. "I love you" as he kissed each of them. "Have a good dream."

Oak Park was one of those upper class towns that drew money and attention far exceeding the population size. There were investment firms, law and professional offices everywhere. They were only a mile from a world-class university, hospital and venture capital buildings. They even had their own hotel, reserved for business meetings and people accustomed to paying $300/night. Karen parked, surprised Justin with a kiss and said, "We're here, but leave that mask on."

Justin obeyed this gentle command hoping that wasn't the last order she gave him. She took his hand, walked into the lobby and stopped. Justin could feel a thick rug under his feet and the sound of people snickering at him. "Could this be someone's house? Is it a surprise party of some kind? Maybe something kinkier?" Or at least his mind went there.

"Thank you" said Karen and she walked him into an elevator.

Justin tried to count the floors, 1, 2, 3 and 4. "We must be in a hotel. She's planned something really hot and wants it to be a surprise."

Ines was visibly relaxed, grateful to have such a good man by her side. Juan never strayed and he always put her and the children before his own needs. They sat on the couch watching television. Ines would put her legs on top of Juan's lap and he would massage them. After a long day on her feet at school, she looked forward to this mini-spa from her husband. It wasn't long before her eyes started to close and Juan found himself watching the show alone.

Karen quietly opened the door, led him over to a bed and sat him down.

Justin thought about taking off his jacket and tie, but resisted. "Maybe she wants me blindfolded the whole time? That would be intense."

Karen put her hands gently on his lapels and said, "Just give me five minutes, ok?" Then touched his cheek.

"It's been five minutes Karen," Justin called out, thinking she was in the bathroom changing. He heard her walking back toward him.

"OK, take off the mask!" Justin heart was pounding a mile a minute now. This was the sexiest rendezvous he had ever had. Now he had to perform up to her expectations. The lights came on and he heard several voices.

"Surprise!" and Justin saw the partners from Karen's firm there, holding champagne glasses and smiling broadly.

"Welcome to the firm Justin" said the senior partner. "We've been holding this room waiting for you to pass the bar. It was starting to get expensive."

Even though Justin knew he was kidding, he was more than a little disappointed in what had happened. A job with the firm was what he wanted, but not what he had been thinking about. He put on his most sincere face and thanked his new boss. "An honor to work for you sir. I won't let you down." He would be working with Karen. He wanted to keep seeing her. "Would that be appropriate now that they worked together?"

A table with fancy desserts, coffee, tea and more champagne beckoned them. Karen, now less personal with Justin, suggested they have dessert and make small talk. "Never too soon to make points at work" she said.

Her change of demeanor hit Justin. "Would this good fortune mean the end of him and Karen?"

Juan and Ines had a great night, as much out of deep love and commitment as passion. It was due in part to the sense of security Juan had, knowing that he had another solid work project to get them through until summer when he had other work he could do. He decided to leave home early tomorrow, stop at church and offer a prayer of thanks for this blessing.

An hour later, the partners pulled out cigars and hard liquor and sat down to play some cards. Karen whispered something to one of them and he acknowledged. He came up to Justin and shook his hand. "See you tomorrow, son. 8:00am sharp you know."

Justin smiled "I'll be there. Thanks again." He and Karen left the room, more like business colleagues than lovers. "Now I understand," said Justin forcing a smile. "You certainly had me guessing. I was thinking."

Karen interrupted "I know what you were thinking" and she led him up the staircase to the fifth floor, stopping at room 502 and opening the door.

"Weren't we just in room 402?"

Karen pushed Justin in and closed the door. "Maybe. I didn't notice" and she started to undress.

"And wouldn't the firm frown on such a thing?"

"Oh, yes" Karen said, "one of us would be fired. But don't worry. They don't know we're in this room." Apparently the danger made Karen even more excited and she didn't hold back any physical or verbal feelings. Justin had the best (and for him at least) the quietest sex ever.

Juan was setting up to move on to the next location, the town hall and courthouse, when he noticed his boss talking to a man in a suit. The man handed him a paper and explained something that his boss was upset about. His boss walked back toward the crew with a dejected expression, tightly gripping the paper.

That morning, Justin got in his car and drove to the firm. His life was better than it was yesterday. No more stress about the bar or getting a job. He passed the Presbyterian Church without noticing. He wasn't sure how he and Karen would turn out but the thought of continuing their relationship in secret created a new challenge. "How do you hide an inappropriate relationship from lawyers who are experts at reading people?"

Karen greeted him when he walked in. "Well, how did your first assignment go?" She said in her most professional tone. Justin patted his attaché case.

"Good, easier than I thought. I gave those workers the injunction and notice of legal action. What idiot wanted to put cobblestones out there anyway?"

The Grand Poobah

"Give me a megabucks ticket," said Joey.

"Only one" said the kid behind the counter.

"You only need one" Joey said "and a pack of lights" motioning to the cigarette picture on the counter. "3, 7, 10, 19, 58 and 83. Good numbers," he thought as he pushed the ticket into his wallet and lit up before he got to the car. Joey's life had been reduced to hoping he could win the lottery, after decades of wasted opportunities and bad decisions.

Joey's parents came from Italy during the great wave of immigrants in the 1920s, opening a grocery store in Newark. Good Catholic boys, they attended Mass twice a week. Joey did whatever his parents asked and did well in school. He was a happy and bright boy. But his father favored Nick, the first-born. "Poppa, why does Nickie get a new suit for church?" he asked.

Joey's father smiled and patted him on the head. "Nickie needs a new suit because he's going to be an altar boy. You'll be one in a few years and then we'll get you a new suit."

But Joey knew it was more than that. Nick got better toys at Christmas and more attention from his parents. Even though he was a better student, Joey would be criticized if he didn't get all 'A's'. Nick would be praised for getting 'B's'.

"Fourth grade is harder than first grade Joey," his father explained. "We'll see how you do then."

Now in his late 50s, Joey looked like Ernest Borgnine, another first generation Italian-American, but without his talent or work ethic. His life more closely resembled Ralph Kramden, the poor bus driver on *The Honeymooners*, wearing a raccoon hat at the lodge. He walked into the Italian-American club and sat down at the card table. "Ciao, come stai," said Joey.

"Bene, bene" replied the other players.

"Give me $300" pulling most of the cash from his wallet and taking his chips.

"Feeling lucky today Joey?" said Mike.

"I gotta believe, Mike, you know that," gambling now his religion.

Joey and his brother Nick worked at the grocery. Nick would be at the cash register while Joey bagged food. One time a tomato slipped from the top of the bag to the bottom, breaking when the customer put it in his car. He returned to complain. His father stared at Joey. "Tomatoes go on top. Give the man a new one and it's coming out of your allowance."

He had joined the Masonic order to make connections for sales. In 1983, the church had reiterated their denouncement of Freemasonry. Rejected by his faith, Joey believed that he was in a state of grave sin, thus justifying the downward spiral his life had taken. His younger son was brain damaged at birth and given up to an institution for life, a common practice in the 1950s; his other son had a compromised pulmonary system, probably related to the smoking addiction he and his wife shared.

"Poppa, I made this for you in art class." Joey handed his father the watercolor with a picture of them both standing in front of the store.

"Where's Nickie and your mother?" his father said. "This is just me and you." *Just.* Joey held back tears.

Eventually, Joey stopped trying to please his father. This led to his smoking, gambling and eating addictions.

Joey thumbed his cards, a 4, 7, jack, queen and king. He looked around the table. "Two cards" he said, then took another cigarette out. In high school, Joey was an all-state lineman. But today, at 5'10" and 300 pounds, Joey was closer to a heart attack than a running attack. "C'mon, give me picture cards" he thought to himself as he looked at his hand. Catching an ace and ten, he now held a straight. "I raise" and he threw $40 in the pot.

Two players threw in their cards, "not with this hand" said one.

Mike glanced over his hand to Joey. "All right. I'll play" and he raised him to $100.

Joey blew some smoke out, looked at his chips; realizing most of his paycheck was on the table. "All in" and he pushed $300 in chips into the middle.

Mike looked at his cards again, checked his wallet, and then gave Joey a smile. "Call." Joey smiled back, laid down his cards and reached for the pot.

A natural talker, Joey had passed up an offer to become the first salesman for a new business venture, frozen orange juice. His gambling addiction and progressive depression kept his wife and son in poverty, even losing a house that his father had bought him years before.

"All hearts" said Mike as he laid down his flush.

A little embarrassed now, Joey finished his cigarette, strained to push away from the table and turned to walk out. "You beat me again Mike."

Walking back to his car, his legs were knocked under him. A punk kid held a knife to his back and took his wallet. "Move and I'll stick you, old man." *Old man.* The youth disappeared down an alley. Trembling, Joey got in his car and drove home.

His wife could tell something was wrong when he came into the kitchen. "What happened?" She said.

"I was mugged. They got my paycheck for the week." Dejected from the theft but glad that he didn't have to tell her about the loss at cards, Joey sat quietly and ate his pasta, then left to watch television. His wife came in from the kitchen. Joey fell asleep, partly from his smoking, obesity and depression, partly from the trauma of being held up. His wife changed the channel, as her show was about to come on when she saw the blonde model reading the numbers for the night.

"3, 7, 10, 19, 58 and 83."

The Devil's Orchestra

"No man chooses evil because it is evil; he only mistakes it for happiness, the good he seeks."
— Mary Shelley

After trying to finesse God for years, Tony finally realized he had been playing in The Devil's Orchestra. The worst part was that he was about to drag his family down with him. Shopping for groceries was now a painful reminder of how much he had lost, but he still spent most of his food money on his daughter.

Unlike his father, who kept him and his mother in poverty by gambling, Tony measured his decisions carefully, knowing his family depended on him for so much. "That will be $38.45 sir." Tony wiped his face and saw that he had $40 left in his wallet as a flush of anxiety ran through him. He tried to hide his concern and handed the cashier the twenty-dollar bills. Walking past the lottery machine, he resisted the temptation of wasting a dollar.

"Is that you Tony?" said his wife greeting him in the kitchen. "Yes dear. There were good prices on fruit, so I got extra. Where's Kelly?" Kelly runs in and hugs her Dad. "There's my princess" as Tony hugs her back and puts on a smile. "How about a snack?" Kelly looked at the bag. "Did you get bananas and grapes?" Her father took out items one at a time. "Hmm, we have lettuce...broccoli...tomatoes...carrots." Kelly stood on her toes trying to peek inside the bag, her smile fading. "peas...cauliflower...string beans." Kelly was pouting now, as her father pulled out the food. "and..oops, here are three bananas and two kinds of grapes!" The ten-year old girl gave a hop and grabbed her favorite foods. "Thanks Daddy," and sat down at the kitchen table. "OK, I'm off to work," said Tony as he kissed them goodbye.

Tony's mind wandered as he drove to the restaurant. His second job helped him keep up with expenses and some food to bring home. He thought if he could just hold on, God would provide some relief. When times were good, he felt blessed; now that his family was struggling, he thought God had turned away from him. "I will do anything," he prayed to himself. "anything to keep my family healthy." Once there was money in the bank, but medical expenses for Kelly drained that quickly after he lost his insurance coverage. At least he had two jobs and his wife's salary as a bookkeeper. Even though they lived frugally, monthly expenses out paced income, making each month a challenge to juggle bills. A comfortable life had been replaced by daily anxiety and stress. There must be a reason.

Sixty-hour weeks were putting a strain on Tony; at 56 he was tired when he came home and had less energy to relax with the family. Tony and his wife saw less of each other too, because of their schedules and child-care. It seemed as though he was slowly draining a gas tank, each week being tougher than the last.

He arrived at work and took his place in the kitchen; Tony's cooking skills kept him employed at two restaurants, though both were 30 hours weekly. He wasn't alone. Multiple part time jobs were common in the economy, allowing employers to avoid paying benefits. Walking out to get his apron, he bumped into Maria, a single mom waitress in her 40s. "Sorry Maria, I wasn't looking." Maria smiled and helped Tony with his apron. "No worries hon....we're all busy here." Tony couldn't help watch Maria as she left. Maria didn't usually flirt with him so this came as a surprise. Tony imagined spending time with her, but quickly snapped out of it, chastising himself for the thought. His wife was devoted and loving, although they had both been too tired and stressed for intimacy lately. As Tony prepared for the dinner rush, he caught Maria in passing watching him. He let out a small smile.

Friday nights were very busy with constant orders rushing in and out of the kitchen, not letting up until 10pm. Waiters and cooks only had time for quick bathroom and snack breaks and by closing only the clean up crew were left. Everyone else left for the night and returned home except for the younger staff that still had energy to go to bars, clubs or a late movie. Tony couldn't remember those days before he was married when you could get by on less money and responsibility. Was he a better person then? Why was life so easy then? Or did it only seem that way? Experience and wisdom should make life easier as you got older, but then there's a turning point where things go downhill, like a bell curve. He realized his best times were behind him.

When he got home, his wife and Kelly were asleep. He dropped into his chair to watch some TV, eat a snack and have a glass of wine. He wouldn't drink at work but a glass of Chianti before bed helped him sleep. He would have to be up early to get to his other restaurant, again missing time with family. Except for church on Sunday afternoon, there were few times when they were all together on the weekend. During the week, his wife worked during the day and Tony worked early morning and nights, leaving them passing by each other.

Tony checked the mail. Several bills were overdue, the worst a notice from the hospital for Kelly's treatments; he could bring the tip money he was saving to them on Monday, explaining that he will keep making small payments. "I didn't hear you come in," said his wife. "Are you coming to bed?" Tony replied with a nod meaning he would be right there. He was thankful for such a good wife, stoically standing by the family and not complaining.

4:30am comes quickly now. Tony takes a shower, kisses his sleeping wife and daughter and heads to his daytime restaurant; he turns on the grills and makes breakfast for himself. By 7am there would be a line waiting for the pancakes and scrambles he makes. He couldn't afford to take his family to this place but there were plenty of people who could and do every day. At least he can bring something home for them to reheat, although the boss kept an eye on how much food he took. His family deserved it. God will provide.

By 2:30 it was time to leave; he made a large scramble and three pancakes to take home. He glanced out to see if the boss noticed. No one was around. He would only have about an hour before he had to go to his other job and wanted to spend that time with family. "Tony, wait up a minute," said the boss. "You know I understand you're bringing that home, but I'm going to have to start charging you something. Food isn't free, you know." Tony felt a flush of panic. He immediately thought of losing this job. "How much," he asked. The boss worked it out in his head. "Well, you have two scrambles at $10.95 each and three pancakes at $8.95. Let's call it $12.00." Tony knew the real cost of food wasn't even half that. Twelve dollars wasn't much to the crowd that ate here everyday, but it was significant to Tony. This weekend meal was a treat for his family and they looked forward to it. "OK" and he handed over a ten and two ones from his tip money. "And I expect you to show me when you take food next time, instead of sneaking out." Tony was really embarrassed now. "Won't happen again boss," putting on a contrite smile. Tony got in his car and drove home, still worried about how to choose between the money and the food he brought home.

Kelly and mom were sitting in the living room watching a kid's show. When Kelly heard her Dad come in, she rushed to the door. "Did you bring pancakes?" Tony smiled, "Don't I always?" knowing now that his decision had been made for him. His wife kissed him on the cheek, rubbed his back and put her head on his shoulder. "You always take care of us." Tony sat down and closed his eyes, taking a short nap while Kelly and mom shared the pancakes. Sleep wasn't restful now. He worried about the day job, finances and Kelly's health. He grimaced and shrugged in his sleep, then feeling someone pulling his arm. "Time to go to work dear" said his wife and he got up and left.

Saturday nights were the busiest here, twice the crowd during the week and more than Fridays or Sundays. This restaurant was so different than the daytime one. People dressed up, the meals were expensive and the dining room had large tables and intimate booths where candles flickered. In the morning, he saw young couples holding hands over pancakes. Here he saw older couples beginning the dance of romance. When was the last time he and his wife had such a treat? Love is for those with no cares or those with money. His life fell outside that circle of happiness, people with means and young lovers, living at home without the stresses that life may bring.

Miguel, his partner in cooking, was preparing sauces for the entrees. "Hey Tony, how's it going?" Tony liked Miguel. He was in his twenties, had plans for getting married and endless energy. Tony wondered if working side by side, the boss would compare them. But Tony was an excellent cook and Miguel complemented his work by getting the sauces and side dishes ready just in time to Tony's entrees so that food could be delivered quickly to patrons. "I'm good Miguel. How's that pretty fiancée of yours?" Miguel's face lit up. "Oh, you know Tony, I'm marrying an angel. After work tonight we're going dancing and even though the guys will be watching her, she's going home with me." Tony nodded. "Keep treating her right and she always will. When's the big day again?" Miguel stirred the three sauces on the stove. "Valentine's Day! It was Andrea's idea. Romantic, but it could be cold." Tony wondered where they could be going on their honeymoon. Miguel offered before he could ask "but Miami should be beautiful then, lots of warm ocean water, good food I don't have to cook and great clubs." Tony patted him on the arm. "Blessings to both of you and a long, happy life."

At least his boss here didn't mind him taking food home. Whatever meats had been around a while were fair for him to make a meal because they received fresh shipments every week, dated in the large refrigerator. His boss made a point of telling customers that they only used fresh ingredients. "Tony, you going to make magic for those people tonight?" said his boss, dressed in his blue suit, white shirt and red tie. "Absolutely, boss, Miguel and I are the magic makers." The boss relaxed. "Great, that's what keeps them coming back. You know we're thinking about expanding the dining room to next door. If we do, we'll need you for more hours. Is that good?" For the first time in days, Tony felt hope. "I'd love that boss. I can work every night if you need me." Tony felt a wave of energy as he continued to prepare the meat entrees for cooking. "And you'll have to do that sooner while Miguel is on the beach in South Florida next month." Miguel smiled. "Let's hope he makes time for the beach," said Tony. They all shared a laugh.

Once it got busy, Tony and Miguel concentrated on cooking, leaving little time for talk about Miguel's honeymoon or much else. They served over 150 people a night here and time went by quickly. The other cooks and kitchen staff looked up to them as they would a head chef in a fine European restaurant, even though this Italian-American bistro was much less pretentious and Tony and Miguel never thought of themselves as better than the others.

Most of the waiters and waitresses here were young, supplementing another job or still in college. Tony knew their time here was temporary and their future was bright. "Wouldn't it be great to start over?" he thought, although he wouldn't trade his wife and daughter for anything. Tony remembered the injustices he had suffered. He would have stayed away from the people who hurt him, politicking for no other reason that he wasn't a college graduate or because of his age. But it wasn't his to judge; everyone has ups and downs. Each person will have to account for his or her actions on Earth. We are only here a short time. Eternity belongs to those who are faithful.

Respect. That's what Tony liked about this restaurant. And if he increased his hours, then he knew he would get health insurance. More money, Kelly's medical expenses and finally, some security! Maybe he would even be able to drop his morning job, especially now that his boss was squeezing him for taking meals home. "I could spend the mornings with my wife, make breakfast for Kelly and take her to school." Tony's sense of hope made him excited and relaxed at the same time.

Tony walked back to the refrigerator to get meat for the first orders. It would take some time to prepare them for cooking, trimming and shaping the cuts and rubbing them with his blend of spices and marinades. Maria was there looking upset. "What's wrong Maria?" Maria turned toward him. "Oh, just a flat tire that I got on the way over. It will be too late to take care of it after work. I'll have to come back during the day on Sunday." Tony knew this meant she would have to take buses home late at night. "Would you like a ride home? It's on my way." Maria seemed relieved. "Oh, that would be great, thanks" and she touched his arm in appreciation. "No problem."

Tony was trimming the fat off the meats to make them just right for cooking. He couldn't help wonder if Maria was looking for more than a ride, remembering the glances she gave him the other night. Suddenly he was imagining dropping her off and Maria reaching over to give him a not so innocent kiss. "Ouch"...he let out as he cut his left thumb. "Serves me right for not paying attention" he thought, justice for thinking this imaginary infidelity.

After he cleaned up, Tony went back to preparing the cuts. He loved his wife. "Why would I even think of cheating on her?" he asked himself. "This is natural, all men think this way. I'm not going to do anything. That would be the real sin." But would it? Tony believed that it was a sin just to have these thoughts, so he felt guilty. "Do these thoughts come from me or from some evil source?" Tony believed in evil, in Satan and in Hell. "This must be him trying to bring me down." His life wasn't stressful enough; now he is being tempted to do something he knew was wrong. "But was it? How could just thinking about something be wrong? No one would know. No one would get hurt."

This was a question he wrestled with all his life. "Is it our thinking or actions that guide our destiny?" He could not identify any great transgressions he had committed; yet his life had gone from comfortable to this fragile state he and his family now endured. Kelly's medical problems certainly weren't her fault; she was an angel. His wife's suffering wasn't her fault; she did the best she could. No, it was when he lost his health insurance, because that company moved out of town, sending the jobs to some other country, which was to blame. Not that Tony thought those people were to blame; they would make a fraction of what they were paying Americans but that would be a blessing for them. "No, the evil is somewhere else, someone set this in motion."

The food was put away, the kitchen was clean and it was time to go home. Maria waited for Tony outside with her hands in her pockets to stay warm. Tony opened the door for her and they left the restaurant. "I really appreciate this Tony. This is no time to be outside waiting for buses." Tony glanced at Maria. "I told you, it's on my way home, no trouble at all." Tony remembered his earlier transgression and had decided that thinking about it wouldn't hurt anybody. "Well, it's more than my ex would do for me. He only cares about himself." Tony pulled up to Maria's apartment building and waited for her to get out. "Here you go, have a good night." Maria squeezed his hand and looked at Tony. "Thanks. I have to pay the babysitter and make sure mine is asleep." Tony wanted to lean over and kiss her. He thought Maria wanted the same thing. He waited, Maria still holding his hand. It seemed like minutes had gone by when it had only been seconds. Maria's eyes glanced downward. "OK, thanks again" and she left slowly and went inside her apartment. Tony could feel his body quivering. No harm done. Time to get home.

Everyone was asleep as usual when he came in. He cleaned up and got into bed. That night he dreamed about what he had secretly hoped would happen with Maria. He woke suddenly at 3am, upset that it had only been a dream. He hoped the dream would continue but it was replaced with a nightmare about losing his job at the restaurant. The next time he woke up, he was glad it was just a dream. It was 4:30am and time to get to his breakfast job.

All that day, Tony thought about Maria and the opportunity that might have been. He wished he had acted on his impulses. What a relief it would be to feel passion again and to be wanted, not just needed. "No, my wife wants me too. It's our life that has ruined our passion, not her, not me." Tony finished the shift, made his scrambles and pancakes and gave his boss the $12. This time the boss didn't give him a dirty look.

Sunday nights were slower at the restaurant, especially in January. The post holiday crowd was always lighter, people spending some time at home or away to some warm vacation spot. Tony patted Miguel on the back. "Hey, young man, how are you today?" Miguel looked upset. "Not sure. I think Andrea may be cheating on me. I was looking at the cell phone bill and saw some calls to her old boyfriend." Tony listened. "It may be nothing. She loves you. Is there any other reason you are worrying?" Miguel paused, and then said "No, just the calls." Tony tried to reassure him. "It's better that you ask her about this. You'll make yourself crazy if you don't and there's probably an explanation for it." Miguel nodded and agreed. He would ask her tonight after work.

Tony worried about Miguel's situation and that it might be just a harmless misinterpretation of the facts. There could be an innocent explanation, or so he hoped. Miguel and Andrea seemed so perfect together. Tony silently prayed for them, believing that might help.

The night continued to go slowly and the boss told Tony and some others to leave early. When Tony got to his car, he saw Maria. "So you got your tire fixed?" Maria nodded. "Yes, luckily it could be patched, so I didn't need a new one." Tony felt himself quivering again and tried to steady his voice. "Yeah, those new tires sure run up a bill." Maria walked up to Tony and whispered in his ear. Tony could feel his heart pounding. "Really, what about your son?" Maria touched Tony on the shoulder. "He's at my mother's tonight" and she gave him a smile. "You remember where I live?" she said. Tony could barely get the words out "Yes, I'll follow you." The four-mile trip seemed to take forever. Tony's heart was pounding and he thought to himself. "What am I doing? This is wrong. I should just go home." But Tony didn't go home.

Walking toward the building, he saw Maria waiting for him. She took his hand and they went up to the second floor apartment. After they got in, Maria took off her coat and put her arms around Tony's neck, kissing him and leaving no doubt about her intentions. Tony was both excited and worried at the same time. What if his wife found out? But how could she? He wasn't expected home for hours and she always retired early with Kelly. With this expectation, he took full advantage of Maria, unbuttoning her blouse while she did the same with his shirt.

Tony drove home energized and excited but filled with guilt. "What have I done?" But knowing that his wife wouldn't find out, he decided that this was going to be the first night of many with Maria. "This is good for me," he thought. "No one gets hurt. It's no different than thinking about it." But Tony was having trouble convincing him of that last point.

The breakfast restaurant was closed on Mondays, so Tony had breakfast with the family before Kelly had to leave for school and his wife go to work. "What did you guys do last night?" he asked. Kelly jumped in "We made play-doh houses and put people in them." His wife added "Yes, we made a little family like ours; we even had them sitting at the table eating breakfast together." For some reason this renewed Tony's guilt so he asked, "Great, what did your family have to eat?" "Pancakes of course Daddy!" said Kelly. "How was your night dear?" said his wife. Tony wondered if his wife knew he got off early. Realizing there was no up side in looking guilty, he put on his best false smile and said "No, same as usual, dinner for the fortunate few." Then Tony dropped his wife off at work and Kelly at school.

Monday he was off from both jobs, but he spent the day wishing he were going in to see Maria again. "Should I call her?" he wondered, not knowing the appropriate first post-affair task. "If I call her, she might think I'm too eager. But if I don't call her, she might think I don't care. Don't care? Do I care? In what way do I care? I'm not going to leave my wife for her, but I don't want to stop seeing her. Wait, I'm not sure if she feels the same about me. What if that was just a one time thing for her? What if she just wanted to see how it felt? Maybe she is feeling guilty too. But why? She's single, nothing to feel guilty about. Unless, she thinks my wife will find out. That would hurt everyone." Tony was realizing that this was becoming more complicated than he thought it would. But he couldn't wait until Tuesday night.

Tony decided not to call Maria. He didn't want to leave an answer on her machine that her son might hear. And he didn't know what to say. He got to the restaurant early, waiting outside for Maria. He had some flowers in his car. "Flowers? What am I doing now?" Maria pulled up beside him and gave him a quick kiss on the cheek. Tony got the flowers and gave them to her. "These are lovely, thank you so much. Do you mind if I put them in my car?" Tony thought that would be best. "That would be fine," he said. "I wanted to call but didn't know if it was the right thing to do." Maria leaned up to him and whispered "I think it would be better if you didn't." Now Tony was confused again. "Was this the end of it? Did his failure to call end it?" Before he could go on, Maria continued, "We need to keep this our secret, ok?" and kissed him again. Tony wanted to take her right there, but knew someone might see them. He held back all his instincts and asked her if he could see her tonight. Maria gave a little pout and said "sorry love, my son is at home but he's going to be out tomorrow at a friend's house." It was clear that Maria wanted Tony as much as he wanted her, but she had the sense to do this in a way that no one found out. Tony was relieved, having imagined that Maria might tell his wife for some reason if things went south between them. "She's very careful. No one will know. No one will get hurt. I wouldn't want my wife to get hurt," thought Tony. Then they went into the restaurant using separate entrances.

"Women can control their passions more easily than men," Tony thought. He couldn't stand the thought of waiting another day, but Maria seemed perfectly at ease with it. Tony muddled through the night, his mind racing with thoughts he shouldn't have while holding sharp knives. He remembered his thumb incident the other day. "Look at her" he thought, seeing her taking orders and calmly talking with customers, "no different than any other night."

Miguel came in a little late, which surprised and worried Tony. Miguel was never late, though this was only 20 minutes. "Miguel, how are things?" he said. Miguel gave a sad look and said. "I took your advice Tony. I sat down with Andrea and asked her about the calls. She started to cry." Tony felt a sinking feeling that his friend's engagement was coming to an end. "But then she told me that the old boyfriend had asked her if he could hold a bachelor party for me...hard to believe, eh?" Tony wished that were the case. Tony prayed that was the case. Only time would tell. Tony decided he had helped enough.

Over the next month, Tony and Maria continued to see each other after work whenever Maria could arrange for her son to be out. Tony hoped this is how it would continue. No expectations, no one gets hurt. Maria felt the same way. "Tony, do your wife and daughter ever go away for the night?" Tony realized this was a golden opportunity. They could be together all night, not rushing out after an hour to cover his infidelity. He began thinking about how he might arrange for his wife and Kelly to be out of town. "Seeing relatives? Surprise mother and daughter trip to Disneyland? Think Tony, there has to be a way." Then he remembered. Kelly was due at the hospital in the city for cancer tests. It would be an overnight trip and mom always stayed with her. "My God, is this what it has come to? My daughter in the hospital with cancer and my using that as an excuse to be with Maria?" Yes, that would work. No one would know. No one would get hurt.

It worked better than expected. Maria arranged for her son to spend the weekend with a friend and even paid for a hotel room for her and Tony. When Tony heard the plan, he realized that his affair had now crossed over into the romantic domain. "What if Maria wanted more than a physical relationship?" But Maria was way ahead of Tony. Not only did she want more, but she had already bonded with him. Kelly and mom's trip to the hospital was on a Sunday after church and they wouldn't be back until late Monday. Sunday at work, Tony and Maria couldn't help giving each other glances. Both knew what the night had in store, all night and the next day too! After work, they took both cars to the hotel (Maria always the careful one), she checked in and set up the room with champagne, dessert and rose petals on the bed. A trip to Victoria Secret was not wasted on Maria, or Tony. He showed up at the room with two-dozen roses and a small silver bracelet in a gift box.

When she opened the door, Tony thought he would explode with passion. They made love, drank champagne, ate rich chocolates and made love some more. Maria seemed more like a woman in her 20s and Tony did his best to keep up. The adrenalin rush was helping. He forgot completely about his wife and daughter in the hospital. This was the relief he had been praying for; God had answered his prayers, just in a different way than he expected. Maria snuggled up close to Tony and whispered in his ear. "I love you!" Tony thought time (and his heart) had just stopped. "What do I say? There is only one right thing to do now and I'm not sure I can do it." He gave her a long, soulful kiss and said, "I love you too."

Tony and Maria decided it would be safe to use the hotel Jacuzzi. It was late and it was open to guests. They were all alone and holding each other, kissing and reiterating those words that Tony feared so much but were hard to resist once Maria had said them. Tony knew he wouldn't have to work in the morning so they stayed up all night, with just catnaps as breaks. Maria seemed very content with the relationship, even though her words implied wanting more. He had to know. But that could wait until tomorrow. No sense ruining the best night he had in the last ten years.

Around 4:00am they both fell asleep, but Maria had set the alarm for 7:30am, with breakfast ordered from room service. Tony was still asleep when it arrived. She quietly set it up in front of the bed, and then woke him up by snuggling close. Maria didn't want breakfast just yet. Realizing this, Tony took her again, Maria being equally passionate. When they finally got around to breakfast, Tony asked, "What time do we have to check out?" Maria told him she arranged for a late checkout, 1pm, while smiling devilishly. They spent that time in bed enjoying every minute. Tony decided to put off his question about her 'I love you'.

Tony had promised his wife he would call to find out about Kelly. He reached her at the hospital. His wife was crying. "Kelly's cancer is returning. She is in surgery now and could be here another week for treatment. I'm staying with her." Tony's heart stopped again, not in joy and passion, but in devastation for his darling little girl. He promised his wife he would make the trip to the hospital immediately and hung up.

Pulling himself together, tears in his eyes, he went to Maria. Maria thought Tony was in love with her and this was going to be a passionate plea to be with her. Tony took her in his arms and whispered, "I have some errands I promised my wife I would take care of before she gets back. Maybe we can get together later tonight?" Maria was excited about extending their time together. "I'll have my son stay with my mom in case you can come over," and she gave Tony a warm hug goodbye.

When Tony arrived at the hospital, Kelly was in the recovery room so he had to wait to see her. He went to the chapel, got down on his knees and prayed. "God, I don't know why this is happening to Kelly. You know she is a sweet and innocent girl. But if you save her, I'll do anything. If this is because of what I have done, I'll stop. Nothing matters except the life of that little girl. Please God, save her life."

Later in the hospital room, Tony and his wife sat with Kelly holding her hands trying to keep her from crying. "It's OK daddy, the doctor said I'm strong." Tony did everything he could to hold it together. "You are strong Kelly and I know you're going to be all right." The doctor came in, took Tony aside and gave him the news. "We think we got it out. Kelly is going to be all right." Tony's smile told his wife that it was good news and Kelly sensing the same, smiled up at her dad and the doctor.

Tony continued his affair with Maria, neither one expecting more than they had started. He kept this secret for the next five years. No one knew. No one got hurt.

Acknowledgements

The 7 Hills Technology Group originally appeared here; it is the sequel to The Da Vinci Diamond.

The Sonoma Murder Mystery * originally appeared in *50 Italian Pastries.*

The Waiting Room * was originally published in the United States by *Apocrypha and Abstractions*, in Australia by *The Fringe Magazine* and in Great Britain by *The Short Humour Site.* It also appears in print in *Daily Flash Fiction 2012.*

The Old Man and the Sea was originally published by *The Piker Press.*

Dream a Little Dream originally appeared here.

Who Stole Asbury Park? * was originally published by *The Piker Press.*

Preheat the Microwave.Com * was originally published by *Leaning House Press* and reprinted by *Scissors and Spackle.*

The Duke of Yelp * was originally published by *Daily Love* and reprinted by *Eskimo Pie.*

Coq a Doodle Do * was originally published by *Bewildering Stories.*

First Love * was originally published in Canada by *The Glass Coin* and in the United States by *Wherever It Pleases.*

Love, Luck and Fate * was originally published by *Daily Love.*

The Bridge Game * was originally published by *The Rusty Nail.*

The Lighthouse was originally published in the United Kingdom by *Alfie Dog Fiction* and in the United States by *The Rusty Nail.*

Respectable Sinners * was originally published by *The Feathered Flounder.*

The Rich are Going to Hell * was originally published by *Weirdyear*.

The Tightrope * was originally published in the United States by *Writing Raw*, in Canada by *Zouch Magazine and Miscellany* and in Australia by *The Fringe Magazine*. It was reprinted by *6 Tales*, *The Piker Press*, *The Legendary* and *Larks Fiction Magazine*.

The Grand Poobah * was originally published in the United States by *Weirdyear* and in Australia by *The Fringe Magazine*.

The Devil's Orchestra * was originally published and printed by *The Chaffey Review Literary Magazine* in June 2011.

- This story also appeared in the collection Trilogies: 18 sets of short fiction.

Made in the USA
Monee, IL
02 April 2024

55562651R10157